Turkish Islamic Architecture

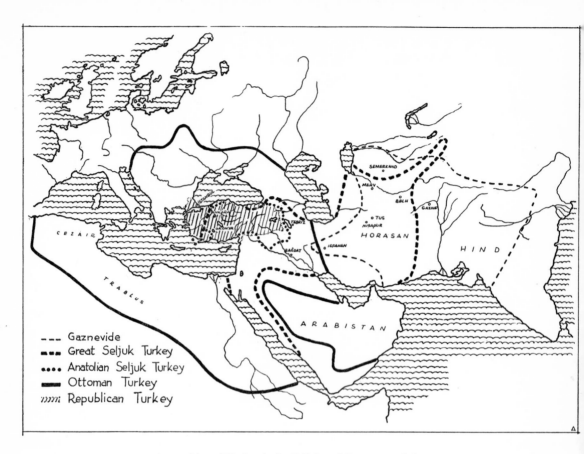

- - - Gaznevide
- ▪ ▪ Great Seljuk Turkey
- • • • Anatolian Seljuk Turkey
- ▬▬ Ottoman Turkey
- 〰〰 Republican Turkey

Map of Turkey in the Seljuk and Ottoman period

TURKISH
ISLAMIC ARCHITECTURE

in Seljuk and Ottoman times
1071—1923

BEHÇET ÜNSAL

Architect, Professor of History of Architecture
at the Academy of Fine Arts, Istanbul

LONDON / ALEC TIRANTI / 1970

PRINTED BY LAWRENCE BROS. (WESTON-SUPER-MARE) LTD. OF WESTON-SUPER-MARE
BOUND BY C. & H. T. EVANS LTD. OF CROYDON

© 1970 ALEC TIRANTI LTD., 72 CHARLOTTE STREET, LONDON, W.1

MADE AND PRINTED IN THE UNITED KINGDOM

ISBN 0 85458 240/1

ACKNOWLEDGEMENTS

For the illustrations I am indebted to the following sources, to which I desire to express my gratitude: Photo Vakıflar: 37, 40, 54, 75, 78, 82, 83, 85, 90; S. Çetintaş (from *Resim ve Heykel Müzesi*): 11, 17, 24, 31, 43, 44, 57, 61, 64, 84, 86, 102, 123; Photo Akademi: 42, 50, 51, 56, 58, 60, 62, 65, 66, 68, 70, 72, 112, 113; S. Ülgen: 59, 79, 95.b, 103; Photo H. Konyalı: 63; Photo Cumhuriyet: 67; Photo S. Jualier: 73; Photo Basın Yayın: 35, 81, 89, 100; Photo Berggren: 101; M. Akok: 106; Photo Sender: 127; from MİMARLIK: 16, 38, 45, 121; from ARKİTEKT: 32, 96; from HAYAT: 124; from BELLETEN: 23, 28; H. Şehsuvaroğlu (from *Istanbul Sarayları*): 114, 115, 117; A. Gabriel: 2; E. H. Ayverdi: 8, 9; Y.K.B.: 128; H. Gluck: 34.

For all other drawings and photographs, I am myself responsible.

I would like to offer my sincere thanks to Professor E. Bean of the University of Istanbul for his great help in the translation of this essay from Turkish to English.

CONTENTS

CHAPTER ONE

CONDITIONS AFFECTING TURKISH ARCHITECTURE

General, Geographical and Historical

Turkish contact with Islam began with the Turco-Arabian conflict of A.D. 642. The first Moslem Turkish dynasty was that of Yasaman Kutay (874). His family lived in the region of Buhara-Horasan and obtained from the Caliph recognition of their independence. The adoption of Islam by the Turkish nation as a whole dates to the years 920–960; but the architectural history of the earliest Moslem Turkish states, such as those of Karahan and Gazne as also of the Turks in Persia and the followers of Tamerlane, are beyond the scope of the present modest volume.

The Turkish adoption of the new religion opened up fresh horizons in both the history of architecture and the history of Islam; the Moslem Turkish armies were destined to maintain the Abbasid Caliphs in power, and later to overrun the whole world of Eastern Islam and the territories of Byzantium.

The mother of Ma'mun and Mu'tasım, sons of the Abbasid Caliph Harun-el-Reşid, was a Turk, and Mu'tasım's personal bodyguard was composed of Turkish soldiers. These, in 832–842, founded for themselves the city of Samarra near Baghdad: from here numerous Turkish commanders overran the provinces of Asia Minor and established independent realms. Later the Seljuks united Western Asia and Anatolia in a great empire under Turkish rule.

THE SELJUKS. Seljuk Bey, of the Turkish line of Oğuz, was an army officer who, with his tribe, migrated from the Kırgız Steppes and settled in Buhara. Tuğrul Bey, one of his grandsons, engaged in war with Mes'ud, ruler of Gazne, conquered Horasan and founded the first Seljuk State in 1040. Subsequently, a number of Oğuz tribes settled in Kars, Erzurum and Malatya, occupied Sivas and reached the Kızıl Irmak (Halys). Tuğrul Bey soon occupied the whole of Persia, which until 1194 remained under Seljuk control; later he overran Iraq and Basra, and in Asia Minor penetrated to the region of Trabzon and Van. On his entry into Baghdad in 1055 he had himself proclaimed Sultan in the very capital of the Caliphs.

Tuğrul died in 1063, and Alparslan, son of Çağri Bey and grandson of Seljuk, succeeded to the power. On August 26th, 1071, the Byzantine army, formed to prevent the growth of the Turks and their expansion into Anatolia, was defeated by him at the pitched battle of Manzikert (Malazkird). This victory opened a new era in the Turkish world. The Georgian power in the Southern Caucasus had already been broken in 1064. Many attempts had previously been made to settle the surplus population of Central Asia in these countries, but they had been opposed by the rulers of Persia; now there was no power remaining to hinder the Turkish settlement of Azerbaijan and Asia Minor.

In 1072 Alparslan was killed. Under his son, Melikşah I (reigned 1072–1092), a start was made towards the occupation of the remainder of Anatolia. Melikşah left the command of the province of Anatolia to Emîr Süleyman, son of Kutulmuş (1071–1086), and conferred on him the title of Sultan. Süleyman overran Western Asia Minor and made his capital at İznik (1080), dividing the control of the new province among his Beys. Thirteen years after the victory of Manzikert Anatolia was a sultanate under absolute Turkish rule.

The great Seljuk Empire extended from Central Asia in the east to the Marmara and Aegean in the west, and from the Caucasus in the north to Egypt in the south. Melikşah's capital was at Ispahan, where the courtyard and dome of the mosque Mescit-al-Cuma are due to him. The Seljuk Medrese founded by his vizier Nizam-el-Mülk (1064–1092), with classrooms and students' quarters round a central courtyard, was the original from which this type of *medrese* spread to Baghdad and Persia. The ruins of the earliest medrese which adopted the *eyvan* system prevailing in the houses of Horasan are in Horasan itself. In this type of medrese, which goes back to the time of Mahmut of Gazne (997–1030), we see an adaptation of the old Buddhist cult to the new religion. The Camai-al-Sultan, which the Sultan constructed in 1092, shows the application of this medrese-form to a mosque. Another new type of

2

building, to be seen on the roads between Horasan and Anatolia, is the sepulchral tower; this is in the form of a Turkish tent, not unlike a pagoda, and was brought to these regions by the Turks.

Melikşah's death at the age of 38 brought a change in the organization of the Empire. His son, Sultân Sencer (1117–1157), established his authority in east and west; his mausoleum at Merv survives in Persia as an impressive monument of Turkish architecture. This high-domed structure, recalling the stupas of Central Asia, was a new type of building which the Turks brought to Persia. After the death of Sencer the unity of the Empire came to an end; in its place we have the Seljuks of Kirman, of Iraq, of Damascus and of Anatolia (Rum); of these, the art and culture of the Anatolian section proved much more lasting than the others. The Arabs called Anatolia Diyarı-Rum (Land of the Romans); similarly the Turks on the continent of Europe called that region Rumeli (Rumelia); this is why the Anatolian Seljuks are known as the Seljuks of Rum.

The following are some of the more important of the Anatolian Seljuk Sultans and their achievements.

Kılıçarslan I (1092–1107) was son of Emîr Süleyman and the first famous Sultan of Anatolia. After the death of the Great Seljuk Sultan Melikşah I he became head of the Anatolian Seljuk State. He it was who not only fought the armies of Byzantium but also opposed the first Crusaders' army in 1095. By the end of these wars the Turks had become the greatest heroes in the history of Islam.

Melikşah II (1107–1116) was a brother of Kılıçarslan.

Mes'ud I (1116–1156) was son of Kılıçarslan. In his time Konya succeeded İznik as the capital city. The Seljuk Sultans of Konya began to bring some of the Anatolian Beyliks under their suzerainty, and abandoning the Great Seljuk kingdom formed the Seljuk State of Anatolia.

Kılıçarslan II (1156–1192), son of Mes'ud, inaugurated the period of development. It was in his time that the Byzantine resistance was finally broken near Konya, and Turkish rule permanently established in Asia Minor. It was he who constructed the monuments known as the Alâüddin Mosque and Pavilion at Konya, who built the walls of Konya (renewed in the time of Alâüddin), and founded the first Seljuk caravanserais. The İplikçi Mosque, also at Konya, is a characteristic structure of his period.

Giyasüddin Keyhüsrev I, son of Kılıçarslan, reigned intermittently from 1192–1210. The twofold hospital and medical school that he built at Kayseri in 1206 in the name of his sister, Gevher Nesibe Hatun, is the first great monument in the history of Turkish medicine.

Izzüddin Keykâvus I (1210–1220) was son of Keyhüsrev. His forces penetrated to the Black Sea and to the Mediterranean, thus opening the world trade route to the Turks. Like his brother he knew Arabic and Persian, and wrote poetry in the latter language. In his time Seljuk architecture begins to assume monumental form.

Alâüddin Keykûbâd I (1220–1235) was brother of Izzüddin. During his reign the process of development was greatly accelerated, commercial relations were established with the Genoese, and exportation was undertaken for the first time. Konya and Sivas both became commercial capitals; between Sivas and Kayseri alone there were erected 24 caravanserais, and at Antalya (Adalia) six khans were built. His new cities, Alâiye (Alanya) and Kubâdiye (near Kayseri) were constructed on the model of the Central Asiatic architectural style, with market gardens, flower gardens and water supply. His sugar factory at Alâiye, and the dockyards on the Mediterranean shore, are noteworthy. The pavilion at Konya belonging to his grandfather, Kılıçarslan II, and his own palaces at Kubâdiye and Kubâd-âbâd (Beyşehir) survive in a ruined state, but his pavilion at Alâiye has not been identified. Other important monuments of his period are the Hatuniye Medrese at Erzurum, with its two minarets, built by his daughter, Hand Hatun, in 1253, and the mosques called Ulu Cami at Sivas and Niğde.

Giyasüddin Keyhüsrev II (1236–1246) was son of Alâüddin. Among the buildings of his period are the Sırçah Medrese at Konya, the Spiral Minaret at Amasya, the hospice of Hand Hatun at Kayseri with mosque, *türbe* and medrese, and the pavilion on the hill of Erkilet.

But by this time the Seljuk Sultans had found themselves obliged to submit to the authority of the Mogul Khans, and later, under pressure from the Ilhanlis, they entirely lost their independence. Nevertheless, even after this, architectural activity did not cease. For example, at Konya the Karatay Medrese, the İnce Minareli Mosque, the mosque and medrese of Sahib Atâ, and at Kayseri the Kılıç Mosque and Medrese, are all of the time of Izzüddin Keykâvus II (1246–1261); from the reign of Giyasüddin Keyhüsrev III (1264–1283) we have the medreses at Sivas and Câcâ Bey medrese at Kırşehir.

4

With the death at Kayseri in 1308 of Sultan Mes'ud II, the enfeebled Seljuk Sultanate came to an end, and the union of Anatolian Turks broke up, the power passing to the hands of a number of independent Beys. The most important of these in the history of architecture are the Beys of Karaman; and their rule, from 1256–1483, was a brilliant successor to the Seljuk civilization. Among many examples we may mention the mausoleum (*kümbet*) of Alâüddin Bey, the medrese of his wife Nefîse Hatun (1382), and the hospice of İbrahim II (1433).

The beylik of Osman Bey was among the smaller of these principalities; yet the Turks under his rule were destined not only to refound the union but finally to create a mighty world-conquering empire, remarkable for its architectural activity.

THE OTTOMANS. The founders of the Ottoman State were Turks of the Kayı branch of the Oğuz family who with their leader, Ertuğrul Bey, came into Anatolia in the time of Sultan Alâübâd Keykûbâd I. Settled by the Sultan in the region of Karacadağ, including Ankara, Konya and Eskişehir, they later took from the Byzantines the district of Söğüt and Domaniç.

On the death of Ertuğrul his son, Osman, succeeded him at the age of 23. Osman Bey was born at Söğüt in 1258. He had at first the title of Uc Beyi (protector of the frontier) under the Sultan, but in 1299, when the Seljuk power was crumbling, he proclaimed his independence. This new Turkish state took its name of Ottoman (Osmanlı) from its founder.

The Foundation Period (1299–1501) begins with Osman the Conqueror. The ejection of the Byzantines from Asia Minor was made complete, and the Turkish forces crossed into Europe, penetrating as far as the Danube. With the defeat of the Crusaders' army the situation in the Balkans was stabilized, and this state of affairs was brought to permanence by the capture of Istanbul in 1453. Bursa, Edirne (Adrianople) and Istanbul were in turn the capital city of the state. The earliest buildings of the period are at Bursa, and their architectural style spread from there to the other cities. This was the origin of that period of Ottoman architecture which we call the Bursa School; the following is a list of some of its principal builders and their works.

Orhan Gazi (1326–1360): Mosque of Orhan Bey at Bursa (1334), the earliest medrese at İznik, the conversion to a mosque of the church of

St. Sophia at İznik.

Hüdavendigâr Murad I (1359–1379): Mosque at Bursa, hospice of his mother, Nilufer Hatun, at İznik, comprising baths, medrese and tiled mosque.

Beyazıt I the Thunderbolt (1389–1402): Ulu Cami and asylum at Bursa, the old Beyazıt Mosque at Edirne, the earliest castle on the Bosporus.

Çelebi Mehmet I (1413–1421): The Green Mosque, the silk market at Bursa, and mosque of the Grand Vizier Çandarlı İbrahim Pasha at İznik.

Sultan Murad II (1421–1446): Medreses and mosques at Bursa and Edirne.

Mehmet II the Conqueror (1446–1481): The original Fâtih Mosque, the Palace (Serai), the castle of Rumeli Hisarı and covered market, the conversion of 12 churches into mosques, the mosque of his viziers, Mahmut Pasha and Mehmet Pasha, the baths of Mahmut Pasha and Gedik Ahmet Pasha and the mosque of Davut Pasha.

The GOLDEN AGE (1501–1703) saw the penetration of the Turkish armies in Europe to the interior of Germany and in Asia to the interior of Persia, the capture of Baghdad and the whole of Arabia and Syria, the occupation of all Northern Africa, and the final determination of the boundaries of the Empire. The Mediterranean had now become a Turkish lake. In this period Turkish architecture attained its final and definitive form; this is the classical age of Ottoman art. During this era Koca Sinan, the great genius of the world of architecture, and his followers filled every quarter of the Empire with the products of their art. We note here a few important items.

Beyazıt II (1481–1512): Mosque-Complexes at Edirne and Istanbul, the two mosques of his vizier, Atîk Ali Pasha, the repair of the Byzantine walls of Istanbul.

Süleyman the Lawgiver (1520–1566): Şehzade and Süleymaniye Mosques, the mosques of his vizier, Rüstem Pasha, and his wife, Mihrimah, mosque of Admiral Sinan Pasha, aqueducts and bridges, the mausoleum of vizier Ayas Pasha.

Selim II (1566–1574): Selimiye Mosque at Edirne, the two mosques of vizier Sokullu Mehmet Pasha at Istanbul and mosque-complexes at Lüleburgaz.

Murad III (1574–1595): Two mosques, the türbes against St. Sophia at Istanbul.

Sultan Ahmet I (1603–1617): Blue Mosque and its appurtenances at Istanbul.

Murad IV (1622–1641): Eminönü Mosque, the tiled mosque at Üsküdar, and the great medrese of Bayram Pasha.

This brilliant period was followed by half a century of stagnation.

From the TULIP PERIOD (1703–1730) dates the beginning of the Empire's decline. The continuous extravagance caused a series of financial crises, and in consequence architectural activity was confined to small decorative buildings. To the time of Sultan Ahmet III nothing can be attributed apart from a number of fountains. Classical Turkish art did indeed survive, as for example under Ali Pasha of Çorlu: but the process of Europeanization had begun. A few pavilions were built in this period by the Grand Vizier İbrahim Pasha.

The TURKISH BAROQUE PERIOD (1730–1808) coincides historically with the period of reform. The Janissaries were abolished. The effects of the French Revolution (1789) began to be felt. Serbia, Greece and Egypt broke away from the Empire and became independent. In the sphere of art, foreign influences began to be prominent. Contact with Europe, the influx of tourists, the effects of the European Renaissance (three centuries late) upon Turkish art—all these caused a total change in the architecture of the period. The Nuru Osmaniye Mosque, built in the time of Osman, son of Sultan Mahmut I (1730–1754); the Lâleli Mosque, of the time of Sultan Mustafa III (1754–1774); the reconstruction of the Fâtih Mosque; the library of Grand Vizier Ragıp Pasha; the türbe and fountain of Sultan Abdülhamit I (1774–1789); the Selimiye barracks at Üsküdar and mosque of Sultan Selim III (1789–1808); these are some of the monuments of the new art. On the other hand, in the mosque of Hekimoğlu Ali Pasha, Grand Vizier of Sultan Mahmut I, we see the old Turkish art living on.

The EMPIRE PERIOD (1808–1867) was a time of reform and revolution in the Empire. The arbitrary rule of the Sultans was brought under restraint by constitutional law. In the military and cultural spheres European innovations were introduced. The türbe of Sultan Mahmut II (1808–1839), the school of Cevrî Kalfa, the Nusretiye Mosque at Tophane, the Beylerbeyi and Dolmabahçe Palaces and Mosques, and the mosque at Ortaköy, are examples of the new style.

In the COSMOPOLITAN PERIOD (1867–1908) architecture begins to decline. In buildings such as the Çirağan Palace and the Valide Mosque at Aksaray, constructed in the time of Sultan Aziz (1867–1876), an eclectic style comprising Greek, Gothic and Moorish elements makes its appearance. Similarly, in the fountains, palaces, schools, banks and administrative offices built under Abdülhamit II (1876–1908), despite the evident desire to create a renaissance of the old Turkish style, a hybrid effect is nevertheless conspicuous.

In the YOUNG TURK (NEO-CLASSICAL) PERIOD (1908–1923) the revolutionary tendencies that had already begun made great advances, and the Turkish Nationalist Movement gained strength. A similar trend is observable in architecture also. The Turkish architects, taking their inspiration from the old Ottoman style, attempted a sort of revival or renaissance, and this continued until the early years of the Republic. But, subsequently, modern international architectural tendencies prevailed. In the latest period of Turkish history the outstanding historical and political event has been the War of Independence and Atatürk's reforms. When, after the First World War, the Ottoman Empire, already falling to pieces, was expected to vanish entirely, Atatürk, organizing the reaction of the Turkish people and leading them to victory in the War of Independence, founded, in 1923 within the national boundaries, a completely new republican State. His reforms have enabled Turkish people to share in the life of the modern world.

In the past the Turkish people have taken various names according to the names of their rulers; thus the names Seljuk and Ottoman are taken from those of ruling dynasties. To-day, however, under the style of Turkish Republic, the Turks are at last called by their true national name.

We conclude these short notes with the words of Atatürk: 'Our State, which is the culmination of thousands of years of Turkish history, has its roots in the social and political necessities of mankind; it possesses every qualification and every condition necessary for stability and permanence'.

Physical Conditions

The climate of Anatolia is, in general, mild but away from the coast it becomes more severe. Whereas in Central and Eastern Anatolia a continental climate prevails, with hard winters and dry summers, towards the south sub-tropical conditions begin; the winters are warm and rainy, the summers very hot and dry. For this reason the buildings have flat roofs. As the ground rises from the south-east towards the north a mountain climate gradually prevails. Western and Northern Anatolia are temperate.

On the Central Persian plateau the winter is very cold and the summer very hot. In the provinces of Horasan and Kirman, and farther south-east in Seistan, the sun's heat is fierce. Mesopotamia and Arabia have a very hot desert climate. These conditions explain why in Anatolia, instead of the open (Hofhaus) system prevailing in the Seljuk buildings of Mesopotamia, Syria and Persia, in similar buildings (mosques and medreses) the closed system is preferred.

Northern Anatolia is rich in timber-forests, and the buildings of this region are of wooden construction. The land midway between east and west, and between the mountains of Northern Anatolia and the Taurus range, form a closed basin 700 to 1,100 metres above sea level. As there are no outlets to the sea the rivers flow into lakes. The steppes of Konya, the centre of Anatolian Seljuk civilization, were once a vast region of lakes surrounded by mountains. Owing to the hot climate these lakes have dried out, but remnants of them are still to be seen. These geological events have left in the district a quantity of such building-stone as lake-limestone and *küfeki*, but more especially clay and mud suitable for bricks. The regions of Sivas and Kayseri are similar. On the hilly plains between Konya and Northern and Western Anatolia travertine and tufa are found. The coasts of the Aegean and Marmara are the home of classical marble. In the time of the Beys marble was used as a facing for brick, in the Ottoman period for the building as a whole. Eastern Anatolia, from north to south, is a region of mountains where stone is the only building material. The white Midiat marble of Mardin and the dark basalt of Diyarbakır are much used in this district.

For this short survey it will be understood why wood and squared stone architecture was adopted in Anatolia in place of the baked or sun-dried brick of Mesopotamia, Turkistan and Horasan. Physical conditions similarly explain why the civic architecture of Tabriz with its abundance of trees, and in general the stone buildings of Azerbaijan, are in some respects different from the Persian style and resemble rather those of Anatolia. Even the conical roofs of the Seljuk mausolea are

9

stone-covered.

The clay and other materials found in their neighbourhood enabled Kütahya and İznik to become centres for the manufacture of tiles; from the territories of these two cities came the tiles employed in the Ottoman Turkish buildings of the sixteenth, seventeenth and eighteenth centuries.

Civilizing Influences

It is an accepted truth that the art and culture of every nation are affected by those of earlier and neighbouring civilizations and the Seljuk and Ottoman are no exceptions.

Investigation of the palaeolithic and neolithic ages in Anatolia has barely begun. What is certain is that the transition to the age of metal was sudden; it is hardly to be doubted that it was due to newcomers from outside, in all probability from Central Asia. This new civilization is exemplified by the Hittites, Phrygians, Lydians and Lycians. All of these contributed to pre-Hellenic art, and the Hellenistic art of Anatolia also owes much to them.

The Early Christian architecture of Syria and Anatolia, and later the Byzantine civilization, arose from the fusion of Hellenistic and native art with the building technique of Sassanid Persia. We have seen above how the Seljuks adapted the Central Asiatic technique and the traditional Buddhist forms to Islamic structures, and how they brought new types from Persia to Asia Minor. Seljuk influence on the Islamic buildings of Persia was very strong.

Until they united under Islam the Turks were in the position of hangers-on to the Buddhist, Manichaean and Christian religions; but when once Islam had been adopted as the national religion they were able to found healthy and homogeneous states. Nevertheless, even in the Ottoman period Turks of the Christian persuasion were to be found in Anatolia. Islam is eseentially a rational religion: it was the Moslem scholars who made the Greek philosophers known to us. With its basic principle that rules must change with time, Islam was no bar to progress in the structure of society. So it was that the Turks were able to incorporate with Islam traditional ceremonies with dance and music, like the Feast of Mares' Milk (Kımızlı Şölen) surviving from the old religions. Hence arose the convents of the Bektaşi and Mevlevi sects. In the rites of the followers of Mevlana Celalüddin-i-Rumî (the

Whirling Dervishes) dance and music play a part. On the Seljuk buildings of the Sunni Moslems decorative sculpture including human and animal figures is still to be seen. In the ornamentation of books also, the Turkish miniaturists made great use of human portraits. Subsequently such representations were strictly prohibited. The practical conceptions of the Seljuks, both in religious and in secular matters, of debarring the Caliph from any interference in politics, brought about a great revolution in the Moslem world. Then for the first time, in 1055, the functions of Caliph and Sultan were separated. Ultimately, Islam, divorced from its character of an Arabic civilization, made possible the development of local and national cultures. The union of the Turks under the Mohammedan faith brought them face to face, in a new country, with Western Asiatic art; but the Turks did no violence to the rites or to the buildings of non-Moslem religions.

Islam prescribes ablution before prayer; this was a great encouragement to the construction of fountains, public baths and water supplies. Similarly, its insistence on education and study from childhood to old age gave a great impulse to the building of medreses. And since social and medical assistance are among the basic principles of religion, hospices and hospitals were required to be built. Finally, the importance attached in Islam to commerce created a demand for hostelries and caravanserais.

In Islam, though great respect is paid to the departed, there is no actual cult of the dead, and tombs do not rise much above ground level. The grand mausolea of certain sultans are indeed contrary to religious ordinances, but they conform to the tradition of pre-islamic Turkish civilization. Religious beliefs were an incentive to the construction of public and social buildings rather than of private dwellings; and the social-political and military situation of the Turks further reinforced this tendency. Even the sultans' palaces consisted merely of a few unpretentious pavilions; and as late as the time of the third Crusade (1190) the Seljuk Sultans lived in tents on the outskirts of the city. Indeed, when city life began in the thirteenth century, it was still their custom to go up in summer to the *yaylas*. This same tradition explains why even the Topkapı palace in the capital city of the Ottoman Empire comprises only a series of small pavilions. Meetings and coronation ceremonies were held in the open air in the courtyards.

11

The Anatolian cities and their Christian quarters that passed into Turkish hands were preserved undamaged but adapted to Moslem requirements. Both in these and in the newly founded cities the Turkish town-planning system, with market gardens, flower gardens and vineyards, was applied. In the foundation of these cities on the Turkistan model, emigrants from that country played an important part. This town planning involved more digging of wells, the opening of canals and the building of bridges. Finally, to meet military needs, town walls, castles, towers and shipyards were constructed. Turkish architecture, in short, has its religious, medical, social, cultural, commercial, artistic, domestic, civic and military aspects.

In the Seljuk State a centralizing feudal system prevailed. At the head of the State was the great sultan; his sons ruled in the provinces as sultans, and in the *vilâyets* as shahs or princes. Each of these princes had independent administrative power, but was subject to the great sultan. This was a continuation of the Central Asiatic 'Ülüş' system of family rule. The administrative, financial, judicial and military affairs of the Empire were in the hands of a privy council composed generally of emîrs (administrative commanders), and presided over by the vizier. This vizier, the arbitrary representative of the monarch, was responsible for the management of all business within the Empire. In the provinces a similar organization, but on a smaller scale, was in force. There was also a consultative council composed of the leaders of the tribes. The funds required for the army, for the sultan's palace, and for all schemes of construction and development, were provided by a powerful financial organization and a wealthy State treasury fed by taxes, agriculture, industry and commerce. In the time of Alâüddin Keykûbâd I the accumulated treasure had swollen to an unusual extent, and his reign is notable for the brilliance of its architectural achievements. Ultimately Konya became a new centre of art and learning, and from all parts of the Moslem world students came eagerly to sit at the feet of the great scholars.

The Ottoman rulers, a century after the foundation of the State, came to be called by the title padishah. All the features of the Seljuk administration explained above were present also in the Ottoman monarchy. At first there was a single vizier; later a number were appointed, with a grand vizier (Vezir-i-Âzâm, later Sadrı-Âzâm) at their head. To him were entrusted the padishah's seal and the general

12

administration. The padishah himself, his viziers, and the rich citizens, spent their swelling fortunes on social and public buildings, for the upkeep and repair of which they also provided various sources of revenue. To use and administer these funds an organization (Wakif) was founded to provide constructional, social and cultural assistance.

Sultan Mehmet II, conqueror of Istanbul, embodied the administrative system in a code of law, and set himself to make the city of Istanbul the legal, artistic and scientific centre of the Turkish Moslem world. This ideal attained its highest realization in the time of Süleyman the Magnificent, who was called the Lawgiver. The wealth that flowed from every quarter of the Empire into the Padishah's treasury was used for developments and constructions of dazzling brilliance; hence the title of Magnificent by which he is known among Europeans.

But from the end of this same sixteenth century onwards the Ottoman Empire began to weaken. In consequence of the sultans' intrigues with the ladies of the Court, their exchange of the old simple life for habits of reckless extravagance, with the resulting financial difficulties, and their disregard of the law, the Empire fell steadily into a decline. Architectural design followed a parallel course.

Excess of population, combined with other historical and political necessities, was constantly drawing the Turkish people from their old homes to the cities of Anatolia. Like every other class, the artists had a guild in every city, whose members were subjected to material and moral control, and were bound to one another by a close professional solidarity. The Ottoman Turks attached these guilds to a central organization. To this is due the strong traditional element, and the purity of workmanship, conspicuous in the various monuments of the various branches of Turkish art. In the large cities the humbler commercial and industrial classes too were organized, while the caravans and international trade were carried on by the capitalist class. To maintain this commerce, roads, bridges and caravanserais were built. The peasants who lived by agriculture or the pasture of flocks and herds had their homes in the villages. For the disposal of this rural produce, as also of commercial goods, market places were constructed in the cities.

CHAPTER TWO

ARCHITECTURAL FORM AND CHARACTER

The fundamental building types in Moslem Turkish architecture are closely connected with its own original tradition. Both religious and secular buildings show the same general structural character but they exhibit a great variety of material, proportion and ornamentation. These buildings may be divided into the following groups:

Religious buildings. Mosques (*cami, mescit*), Convents (*tekke*), Mausolea (*türbe, kümbet*), Tombs.

Secular buildings. (a) SOCIAL AND PUBLIC: Schools (*medrese, dar-el-kırae, dar-el-hadis, dar-el-sıbyan*), Hospitals (*şifahane, bimarhane, tabhane*), Hospices (*imaret*), Hostelries (*han*), Caravanserais, Market Halls (*arasta, çarşı*), Public Baths (*hamam*), Public Fountains (*sebil, çeşme*), Aqueducts, Reservoirs, Bridges:
(b) DOMESTIC: Palaces, Castles, Houses, Shops.

Military buildings. City Walls, Towers, Forts, Barracks.

Form and character vary not only in the different types of building, but also according to style and period. The following are the main periods in Seljuk and Ottoman Turkish architecture.

SELJUK STYLE
A.D. 1040–1194. Great Seljuk (Persian) Period.
A.D. 1071–1308. Seljuk Anatolian Period (Rumî).
A.D. 1256–1483. Beylik Period.

OTTOMAN STYLE
A.D. 1299–1501. Bursa (Early) Period.
A.D. 1501–1703. Classical Period.

A.D. 1703–1730. Tulip Period.
A.D. 1730–1808. Turkish Baroque.
A.D. 1808–1908. Cosmopolitan Period.
A.D. 1908–1923. Neo-Ottoman Period.

In the present short essay, space will not permit us to examine separately, with examples, the character of every type of building in all its styles and periods. We must be content with analysing the plan and structure of the principal religious and secular building types only and noting the characteristic changes in style in the various periods.

Mosques

Among the Moslem Arabs the building in which communal prayer is performed is called *mescit*. From the Arabic pronuniciation of this word, *masgit*, the name Mosque is supposed to be derived. Among Moslem Turks *mescit* means a small mosque; the larger buildings are called *Cami* (*Djami*), that is, a place of assembly. And in practice a mosque is not merely a place for prayer (*namaz*), but also for listening to the Koran, to the Mevlud, to sermons and to addresses. There are also in other Moslem countries buildings called *Mescit-i-Cuma*, in which State proclamations and official announcements are made, and in which the Friday service is conducted. Let us examine the course of their evolution.

Seljuk Anatolian Period. The plan and structure of the mosque is similar to that of the early Moslem mosques.

The earliest Arabic mosques are known to have consisted of an open court surrounded by a wall and covered portico (*zulla*) with flat wooden roof supported on wooden posts, as in the mosques of Fostat and Kûfa. This multi-pillared Arabic system is influenced by the Abadana of Persepolis and the hypostyle chambers of Egypt. In the İbni Tulun Mosque at Cairo, built by a Turkish governor in 879 arcades on pillars are used as supports in place of wooden columns, and are arranged parallel to the central axis. In the Great Mosque at Cordova (787) the arcades are built across the line of the central axis. If we add that in the Great Mosque (Camii Kebîr) at Damascus and in the Al-Azhar Mosque at Cairo the centre aisle was wider than the others (see Creswell), we shall have indicated briefly the general scheme of the earliest Moslem mosques.

15

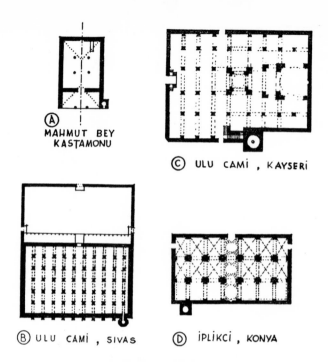

1. Sketch plans of Seljuk mosques

The Turks first applied this plan in the case of the Samarra Mosque (852), and in Anatolia the Seljuks modified it to suit the climate, giving it generally the name of Ulu Cami. They began by closing the open side of the zulla facing the court; in this way a plan with pillars and all four sides enclosed came into fashion. Eventually the courtyard element of the Arabic mosque was, in general, dispensed with; but its memory survives in many places, where a part of the roof in the line of the central row of columns was left open to the sky, and the fountain (*şadırvan*) placed under this opening: the Ulu Cami at Erzurum, a work of the Saltuks (1179), and the Seljuk Huand Mosque at Kayseri (1237), are examples. The building at first had a flat wooden roof supported on wooden colums, and this type long survived in the forest region and its neighbourhood, as for example in the mosque of Mahmut Bey at Kasaba near Kastamonu (1366). In this mosque the detail of the wooden piers, rafters and ceiling, and the coloured designs upon them, are equally attractive. The oldest specimen of this type that has survived to our time is the Ulu Cami at Afyon, dating to 1272; its walls are of stone; the intercolumnar space is 3·70 m., and in the central row 5·10 m.

ıa, 39

16

In this way the Mecca axis is emphasized; the rafters are at right angles
to this axis. An interesting feature in the Eşrefoğlu Mosque at Beyşehir
is that in front of the *mihrab* is a dome, and in the middle a hole in the
roof to admit light. Later, the stone columns or pillars were joined by
stone arches, but the building continued to be roofed with a layer of
earth upon horizontal wooden rafters; the Ulu Cami at Sivas, supposed   1b
to be the oldest mosque in Anatolia (eleventh century), is of this type;
its minaret, however, is of the thirteenth century. As in the case of the
mosque just mentioned, in the Danişmend Ulu Cami at Kayseri (1140)   1c
the axis of the mihrab is further defined by two domes, one of which has
a light-aperture. This must be considered an advance in planning
technique. The history of Anatolian Seljuk architecture begins later
owing to the wars with Byzantium and with the Crusaders, and to the
founding of a unified national State. The Alâüddin Mosque at Konya   35
dates from 1156–1220, and is roofed with a layer of clay over wooden
rafters resting on arcades supported by columns across the width of the 36a
building. Its original simple geometric plan is obscured by later additions; the minaret in fact stands on one of these. The courtyard wall containing the gateway, built by Mehmet Bin Havlan of Damascus, is
under Syrian influence; but the conical roof of the türbe, and the manner
in which the square plan of the main mosque is combined with the
circular drum of the central dome by means of triangular surfaces, as   36b
also the mosaic tiling, are purely Seljuk Turkish; these are the work of
Ömer Yusuf of Haraç. An inscription on the pulpit tells us that this
part was built in the reign of Kılıçarslan II, whose vizier built the
İplikçi Mosque at Konya. This mosque, which Sarre was unable to see,
was not repaired and opened to the public till 1938. It is constructed
entirely of stone, and the number of internal piers is reduced to twelve;
the arcades run in both directions and support vaulting; in the central 1d
section are three oval or spherical domes. In view of the date of this
mosque (1162), and bearing in mind that in the earliest Anatolian
mosques the call to prayer was made from the roof, the fact that it
contains the base of a brick minaret is deserving of attention. The Ulu
Cami Mosques of Urfa and Niksar have a similar character; the latter,
at Tokad, is the older (1145), and has buttresses in the outer walls
supporting the vaults. A more developed form of this same plan is to be
seen in the mosque of the Spiral Minaret at Amasya (1237–1247) and in
the mosque of Hacı Kılınç at Kayseri (1250), and consists in the widen-

17

ing of the central aisle and the reduction of the number of pillars. The Hisar Mosque at Divriği, with six pillars, dome and vaults, is still older (1180), but must be reckoned a Mengücük Turkish building.

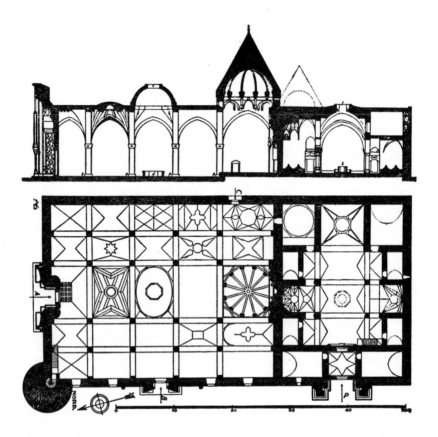

2. Plan and section of Ula Cami and Mental Hospital, Divriği

2 The richest and most impressive of the Seljuk mosques at Divriği, the Ulu Cami (1229), is of similar plan and structure, but differs in
37 having 16 pillars and ribbed vaulting. Adjoining it is a hospital (*şifaiye*). The Seljuk architects, by reducing the number of pillars in this type of mosque to a minimum, afforded a model for the Ottoman Ulu Cami.

Beylik Period. The principalities (*beylikler*) that succeeded the Seljuk rule were sixteen in number. Here we can only select a few examples that display some contribution to evolution in design.

18

The early fourteenth-century mosques of the Çandar family at Kastamonu and the Eşrefoğlu family at Beyşehir, with their wooden pillars and roof as described above, repeat the earliest Seljuk type of building. And similarly their stone-built Ulu Cami Mosques show a parallel development to the Seljuk type; the Arapzade Mosque at Karaman (1374–1420), the mosque of Taşkın Pasha at Ürgüp, and the mosque of Sungur Bey at Niğde (1335), are examples.

The Ulu Cami mosques of the Artuk district around Malatya, Diyarbakır and Mardin are in the form of an oblong wider than it is deep; their special character consists in the arrangement of the pillars in two or three rows, and the large egg-shaped domes set on pendentives at the eight corners in front of the mihrab. These mosques date to the twelfth and thirteenth centuries. Some of them have also a courtyard.

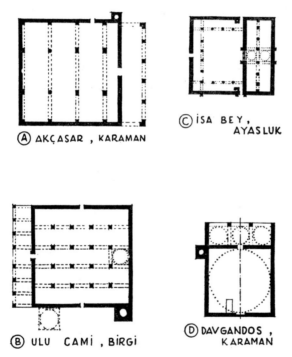

Ⓐ AKÇASAR , KARAMAN

Ⓒ İSA BEY , AYASLUK

Ⓑ ULU CAMİ , BİRGİ

Ⓓ DAVGANDOS , KARAMAN

3. *Plans of various Beylik mosques*

In the fourteenth century an innovation was introduced in the form, first of a portico in front of the mosque, as in the Akçasar Mosque at Karaman and the Ulu Cami at Birgi; then of an interior court, as in the

3a

3b

19

3c Ulu Cami at Manisa and the mosque of Isa Bey at Ayasluk (Ephesus). This last, by discarding extravagant decoration, shows a transition to the pure and simple style of the Ottomans. Another new mosque-type has a square interior surmounted by a large dome, and a portico (*son cemaat*
3d *yeri*) in front with domes above, as in the Davgandos Mosque at Karaman. This plan is important as furnishing a prototype of the Ottoman mosque.

Ottoman Period. Under the Bursa School, the Ulu Cami type continued both in Istanbul and in the provinces, but with this difference, that the
4a roofing consists of co-ordinated domes. Specimens of this type are the
4o, 41 Ulu Cami at Bursa (1394–1399) with 20 domes and 12 piers, and the
4b, 50 Eski Cami at Edirne (1404–1414) with nine domes and four piers. As in the Seljuk mosques, one dome in the central axis is open at the top, and in some cases there is a waterbasin below this. This plan, employing the minimum number of domes and piers, is preserved at Istanbul in the
4c fifteenth-century mosque of Zincirlikuyu and the sixteenth-century mosque of Piyale Pasha. Later, however, this type, being found unsuitable for a mosque, was abandoned, and came to be used rather in secular halls. To this period too, beginning in the fourteenth century, dates the development of the mosque with a single dome, such as the
4d, 4e Alâüddin Mosque at Bursa (1326), the mosque of Hacı Özbek (1333)
42 and the Green Mosque (1378) at İznik (the latter a very splendid monument), and the mosque of Mahmut Çelebi (1443). There are in Istanbul still finer specimens of this type, as for example the mosques
4f of Firuz Ağa (1491), Bâli Pasha (1504) and İbrahim Pasha (1551). The Kurşunlu Mosque at Kayseri (1586) closely resembles that of İbrahim Pasha. There are differences of technique: at Bursa and İznik the transition from the square plan to the round dome is effected by triangular surfaces, at Istanbul by means of pendentives; and there are differences in architectural effect; at Istanbul the front arcade is kept low and is in the nature of an addition to the main building, whereas at Bursa and İznik it rises with the mass of the main structure. In the mosque of İskender Pasha at Ahlat (1568) the dome has pendentives, but the general plan belongs to the Bursa School. From the middle of the fourteenth century a third type, developed especially at Bursa, makes its appearance. This comprises a central *sahn*, three eyvans (one in the main axis, two in the cross-axis), small rooms, and an incomplete upper storey containing

20

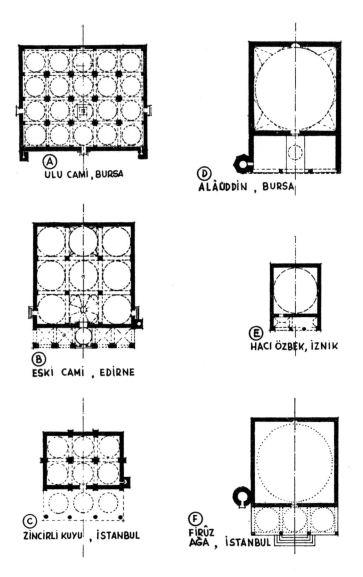

A ULU CAMİ, BURSA

D ALÂÜDDİN, BURSA

B ESKİ CAMİ, EDİRNE

E HACI ÖZBEK, İZNİK

C ZİNCİRLİ KUYU, İSTANBUL

F FİRÛZ AĞA, İSTANBUL

4. Typical plans of early Ottoman period mosques (type I-II)

other rooms. The eyvans are raised two or three steps above the ground level and are generally roofed with a dome or vault; the central one is used for prayer. This is the arrangement in the mosque of Murad I (1363) 5, 43 and the Yıldırım Mosque (1390) at Bursa. Above the central area which 45, 6b takes the place of the courtyard is a light-turret surmounted by a cupola, with a water-basin below, as in the Green Mosque at Bursa (1421). 7

21

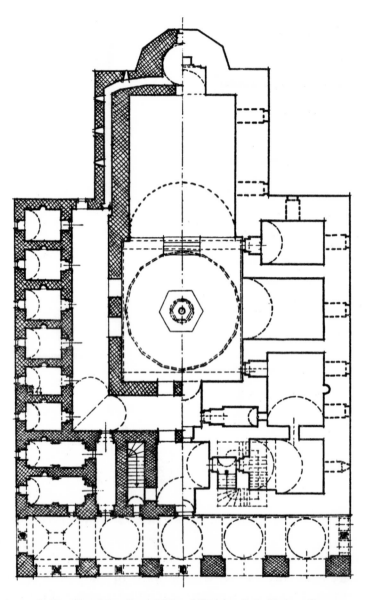

5. Ground and first floor of Murad Hüdavendigâr Mosque, Bursa

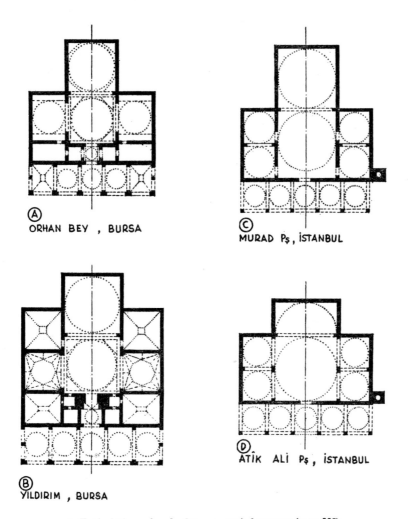

(A) ORHAN BEY , BURSA

(C) MURAD Pş, İSTANBUL

(B) YİLDIRIM , BURSA

(D) ATİK ALİ Pş , İSTANBUL

6. Typical plans of early Ottoman period mosques (type III)

This type of building is not a pure mosque type, but is properly a **46-49** secular building combining the functions of mosque and medrese. Indeed, we actually find this plan adopted in the Câcâ Bay Medrese **14b** at Kırşehir (1272) and other Seljuk medreses containing eyvans. The same plan has been used earlier in the time of the Great Seljuk Sultanate in the Mescit-al-Cuma at Ispahan (1072), and was repeated by the Turks in Egypt in the Mameluke Mosque of Sultan Hasan (1356). In Anatolia, as we saw above, the central court was for climatic reasons covered over by a lantern cupola; this plan was first used in the mosque

23

of Orhan at Bursa, and later in Edirne and other provinces, and at
Istanbul in the mosques of Mahmut Pasha (1464), Murad Pasha (1466)
and Atîk Ali Pasha (1498). In this last the effect of spatial unity, already
observable in the Üç Şerefeli Mosque, is enhanced by the addition of a
half-dome supporting the main dome in the line of the central axis.
This plan, with one dome and one half-dome, before being used in
Istanbul, had already been applied in Anatolia in the mosque of Yahşi
Bey at Tire (1446). In the mosque of Beyazıt II the central dome is
supported by two half-domes—a plan reminscent of that of St. Sophia.
Nevertheless, the numerous architectural differences remind us that the
Turks had applied this technique and this form since Anatolian times,
and were only bringing to its ultimate evolution a building style that
was traditional to them. The Byzantines had found the model for
their half-dome in the buildings of ancient Rome and Syria, and the
Turks, before they had reached Byzantium, had seen this form in
Syria, and used it in their own buildings.

Before we come to the sultans' mosques of Istanbul, we must consider the Üç Şerefeli Mosque at Edirne (1438–1447). Here we see
distinct technical advances: a narrow oblong with two pillars, the centre
covered by a large dome over a hexagon and each side by two domes; in
front, a peristyle court. This inspired plan was the prototype of the
sultans' mosques.

The first Sultan's Mosque at Istanbul was that of Fâtih Mehmet II;
built in 1463–1471, it survived until the middle of the eighteenth
century; the present mosque that has taken its place is built upon a
different plan modelled on that of Sultan Ahmet. Investigation has
shown that the original plan comprised one whole and one half-dome,
as in the mosque of Atîk Ali Pasha; and this same plan was later repeated
in the Selimiye Mosque at Konya (see Riefstahl, ART BULLETIN XII,
1930). The present courtyard survives from the original building, and
is a variation of the type seen in the Üç Şerefeli Mosque.

We may now consider the mosque of Beyazıt II at Istanbul (1501–
1506), which set the pattern for the monumental mosques of the
sixteenth century. Here the plan of the Fâtih Mosque has been developed, and a further step forward has been taken, namely the introduction of a second half-dome opposite to, and in the same axis with,
the half-dome that supports the central dome on the side of the mihrab.
This is the principle on which Koca Sinan, genius among architects,

24

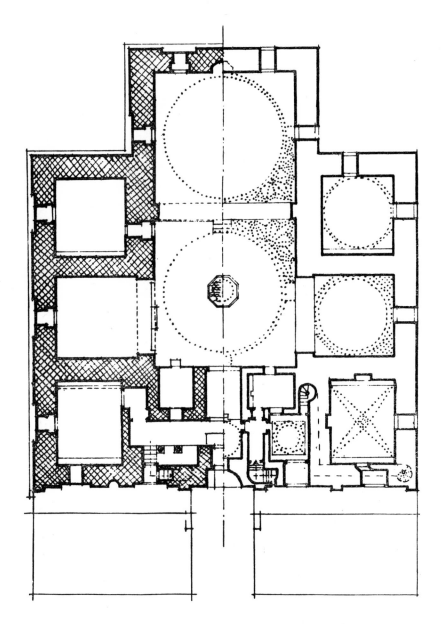

7. *Ground floor and half floor of Green (yeşil) Mosque, Bursa*

c

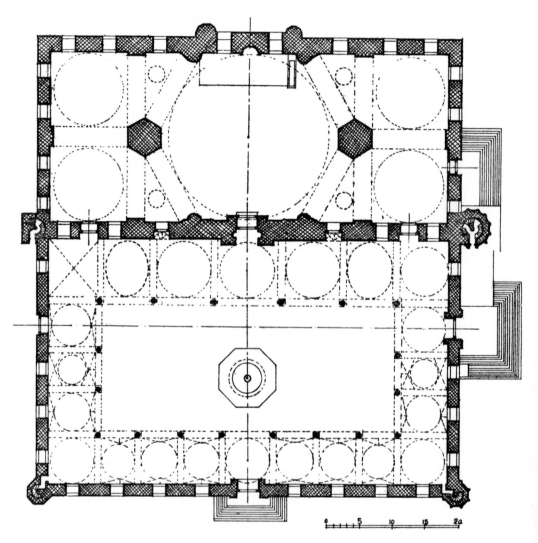

8. *Plan of Üç Şerefeli Mosque, Edirne*

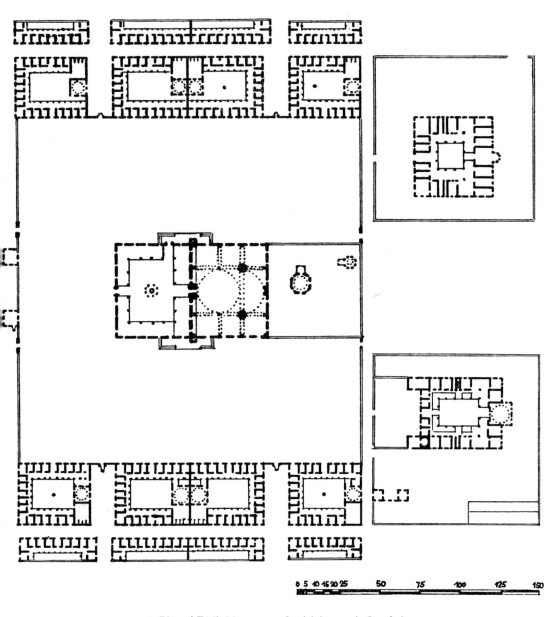

0 5 10 15 20 25 50 75 100 125 150

9. Plan of Fâtih Mosque complex (civic centre), Istanbul

27

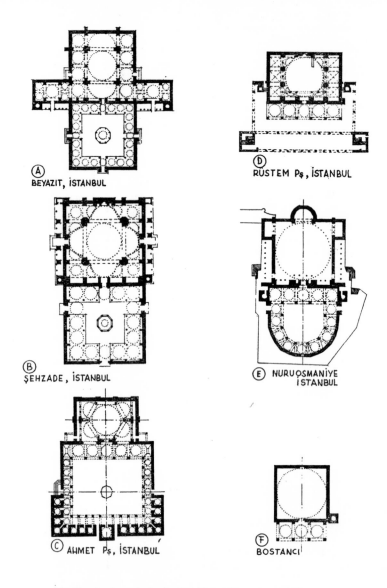

Ⓐ
BEYAZIT, İSTANBUL

Ⓑ
ŞEHZADE, İSTANBUL

Ⓒ AHMET Pş, İSTANBUL

Ⓓ
RÜSTEM Pş, İSTANBUL

Ⓔ NURUOSMANİYE
İSTANBUL

Ⓕ
BOSTANCI

10. Sketch plans of classical and later Ottoman period mosques

28

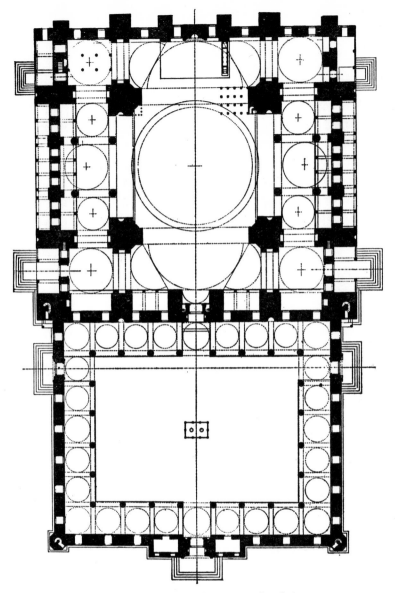

11. *Plan of Süleymaniye Mosque, Istanbul*

designed his masterpiece, the Süleymaniye Mosque (1550–1557). At ıı, 60-62
an earlier date he had experimented with these two supporting domes in
the cross-axis also, namely in his first great work, the Şehzade Mosque 57, ıob
(1543–1548). The plan of the Süleymaniye Mosque, as we have seen, 58
is found earlier at Istanbul in the mosque of Beyazıt II; that of the

29

Şehzade Mosque on the other hand—a central dome surrounded by four half-domes—has its forerunner not in Istanbul but at Maraş in the county of the Dulkadir family, namely the Ulu Cami at Elbistan repaired by Alaüddevle in 1479–1515.

Turkish architects worked for a century and a half on this type of building. The master himself, when he began his design for the Şehzade Mosque, aimed at giving monumental form on the lines of the old Turkish buildings he had seen in his youth, and while introducing innovations to the capital, yet maintaining ties with tradition. Sinan had observed the interior unit of the Üç Şerefeli Mosque at Edirne, with its single central dome, built 100 years before his time. Adopting its plan with modifications, he built in Istanbul a number of mosques having a dome resting on a hexagon or octagon: for example, the mosques of Sinan Pasha, Ahmet Pasha, Sokullu Mehmet Pasha, Mihrimah and Rüstem Pasha. His aim was to apply on a monumental scale, and to bring to its full completion, the early type of small Turkish Mosque with a single dome. This he successfully achieved in another of his masterpieces, the Selimiye Mosque at Edirne (1569–1575). How firmly attached he remained to the traditional ideal is seen from the fact that he later repeated the experiment in some of the viziers' mosques that he built in Istanbul.

The architects of the seventeenth century made fresh experiments on the plan of the Şehzade Mosque, as may be seen in the Sultan Ahmet Mosque (1609–1616) and in the New Valide Mosque at Eminönü (1597–1663).

In the eighteenth century a change of style becomes apparent; nevertheless, the influence of classical Turkish architecture continues for a time, to be felt as in the mosque of Hekimoğlu Ali Pasha (1734). In the Nuru Osmaniye Mosque (1755), a specimen of Turkish Baroque, the new style is seen in the minor architectural features and in the detail, while the general plan, with single central dome, remains faithful to the old Turkish tradition. In the Lâleli Mosque of the same period (1763) Sinan's octagonal plan is still to be seen, although there is a difference of style.

The mixture of style in the small single-domed mosques of the nineteenth century is a reflection of the general crisis which the architectural world underwent. The break with tradition went so far that we even find, in the Dolmabahçe and Ortaköy Mosques (1853), Corinthian

30

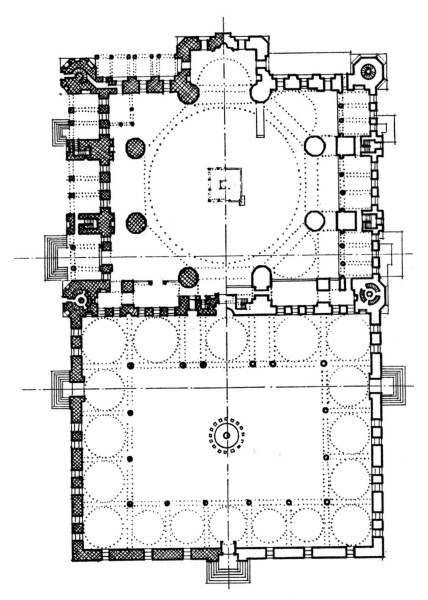

12. Ground and gallery floor of Selimiye Mosque, Edirne

columns and capitals introduced into the design of the minarets.

10f, 73 In the early twentieth century Turkish architecture returned to its own classical style. The mosques of Bostancı (1913) and Bebek (1915), which are on a small scale, have a single dome resting on pendentives in the manner of the Ottoman Bursa School.

Medreses

The medreses were institutions for advanced education, corresponding to the University Faculties of our own time, where the various branches of learning were taught and studied. In addition to the theological schools there were others where mathematics, geometry, astronomy, medicine and other exact sciences were taught. The Seljuk and Ottoman rulers, anxious to spread learning as well as the precepts of Islamism, founded these institutions all over Turkey. With the same objects in view, students coming from a distance were not only provided with free board and lodging, but were also given a monthly allowance in cash. To provide for the students' lodging and for their studies, rooms with fireplace and cupboards, a communal classroom and mescit, a professors' room, a library, and sanitary arrangements were installed on one or two storeys around a courtyard; these arrangements determined the form of the building. This plan does not include a kitchen; meals were obtained from a public cookhouse. The medreses are architectural monuments of civilization and learning no less important than the mosques. The earliest examples are the State medreses built at Nishapur, Tus and Baghdad by Nizam-el-Mülk, vizier of the Great Seljuk Sultan Alparslan and his son Melikşah, together with other medreses of the eleventh century in Merv, Balkh and Herat. The Gazne medrese at Nishapur, called Sâdîye, is still earlier. The origin of this type was briefly discussed in the historical introduction above.

Anatolian Seljuk Period. The plan first employed in Persia by the Great Seljuks, comprising four eyvans set in the two axes of a courtyard, is of great importance in the history of architecture, furnishing as it does the prototype of the mosques and medreses of Turkistan, Persia and the Ottoman Empire. When the Seljuks introduced this design into Anatolia, they applied it in two forms, depending on whether the central court was, in conformity with climatic requirements, left open to the sky or covered with a dome. In the latter the domes, having, like those of the

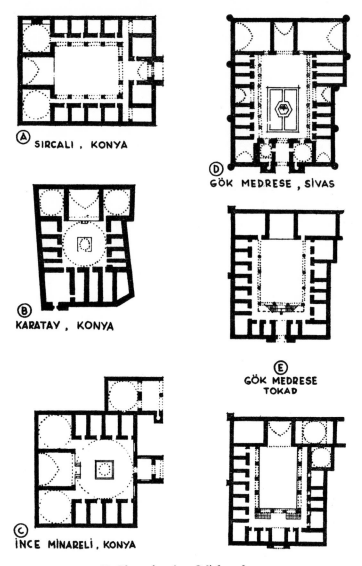

A SIRCALI , KONYA

B KARATAY , KONYA

C İNCE MİNARELİ , KONYA

D GÖK MEDRESE , SİVAS

E GÖK MEDRESE TOKAD

13. Plans of various Seljuk medreses

mosques, a lantern for the admission of light and a water-basin beneath, continue to give the impression of a courtyard. In certain Seljuk medreses we find a further feature which is not without effect on the building as a whole, namely a small mosque for public use containing the mausoleum of the founder. This explains the minarets which strike the eye in many Seljuk medreses. The ruined medrese of Yağı Basan at Tokad (Niksar),

33

built by the Danişmends in 1157, of which only the walls are standing to-day, is one of the earliest. Notable features are the vaults with pointed arches, the double eyvan and central dome, the entrance placed to one side, and the rubble construction.

13a   Two buildings at Konya, the Seljuk capital, may be quoted as characteristic specimens of the two types mentioned above. The Sırçalı Medrese (1243) has an open courtyard and is completely symmetrical in plan; pointed arches and cross-vaults are also used in its construction.
74 The glazed bricks (sırça), which give the building its name, cover
75 the walls of the eyvans with coloured geometric designs. The stone gateway is decorated with sculpture.

13b   The Karatay Medrese (1252) on the other hand has a lantern cupola over the central court. The coloured tiles which decorate the walls of the eyvans and the interior of the dome are especially fine. The marble
76 decoration of the gateway, the use of a lintel in place of an arch over the door, the almost square form of the gateway as a whole, and the position of the entrance not in the axis of the building but on one side, are features that distinguish this masterpiece from others.

13c   The İnce Minareli Medrese (1258) is a theological school. It is similar to the Karatay Medrese, but has a symmetrical plan with centrally placed gateway. The interior of its lantern dome is faced with glazed bricks arranged in patterns. The four corners of its central hall pass by
78 means of fan-shaped consoles with triangular surfaces into a 20-sided polygon, and this in turn into the circular dome. This combination, which occurs also in the Karatay Medrese, is an entirely original Turkish device. The partially ruined minaret of glazed brick which now
77 rises beside the ornamental gateway belongs to an earlier mescit with single dome. This was an independent building; the method of its incorporation in the medrese is similar to that in the Taş Medrese at Akşehir (1250). This latter has the form of a courtyard in the long axis; its minaret gives an excellent idea of Seljuk minarets in general.

After Konya, Sivas became one of the Seljuk capitals. By reason of the city's political and economic importance it contained the largest of all the Seljuk hospitals (1217), a mental hospital which was at the same time a medical school. This explains its form, which is that of a double medrese. The hospital section survives, but in a ruined state; the plan
14a is that of a medrese with courtyard. Its founder, Izzüddin Keykâvus I, was by his own wish buried here. In the tile decoration of his türbe

34

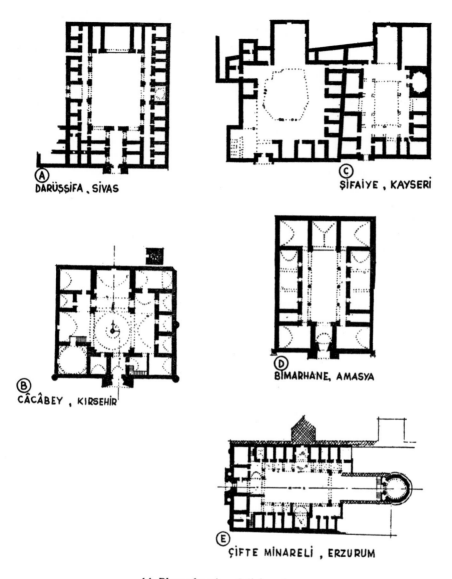

14. Plans of various Seljuk medreses

Hittite themes occur. This, and the two female heads and marching lion in relief in the open-air schoolroom and on the arch of the gateway, are interesting and important features. In fact, similar sculptured figures occur in many Anatolian Turkish monuments of the Middle Ages. The Çifte Minare, Büruciye and Gök Medreses at Sivas were by a coincidence, all built in the same year (1271–1272). The Çifte Minare is a theological school founded by the İlhanlıs. To-day the front alone is standing; its decoration is ornate but clear and harmonious. The

13d Gök Medrese has the same plan. Over its marble gateway are symbolic
81 reliefs in the form of animals' heads; on either side is a minaret constructed, like the dome of the mescit, of glazed brick. The courtyard is bordered on each side by arcades; the water-basin in the middle and the tall poplar trees give the building a most picturesque interior.

13e   The Gök Medrese at Tokad (1275) also owes its name to the sky-blue colour of its tiles; it has two storeys. A striking feature is the gallery which surrounds the court.

14b, 82   The Câcâ Bey Medrese at Kırşehir was built about the same time (1272). The arrangement of this combined mosque and medrese, with eyvans on three sides around a central hall with dome open at the top, is reckoned to be the prototype of the early Ottoman buildings at Bursa.

Another capital city was Kayseri. Here nine medreses are still standing, but like all Seljuk buildings they are in ruins. One of them,
14c the Giyasiye or Şifaiye Medrese (1206), is a very early hospital and medical school.

14d, 80   At Amasya, the mental hospital of Melîke Yıldız Hatun (1309) has the form of a single small court-medrese: its walls of squared stone blocks are well preserved. Its dormitories, forming a long gallery, are roofed with pointed vaults.

14e, 79   The Hatuniye or Çifte Minareli Medrese at Erzurum, built in 1253 by Hand Hatun, daughter of Alâüddin Keykûbâd, possesses some unusual features. It has four eyvans, interrupting the arcades of the courtyard; both arcades and eyvans are two storeys high. It has a round türbe, placed at the back of the eyvan at the end of the long axis. The front, with gateway and two minarets, anticipates the style of the Gök Medrese at Sivas. It apparently occupies the site of an earlier building of the Saltuk period.

Beylik Period. In this period the plan and design of the Seljuk medreses continues to be applied without change: there are, however, certain differences in the architectural features and decoration. The Tol Medrese at Ermenak (1339), now in ruins, is of rectangular court-medrese type. A striking and novel feature is a small window over the segmental arch of the entrance gate. At Karaman, the Hatuniye or Nefîse Sultan Medrese (1382) is a work of the architect Lokman Bin

Hoca Ahmet. The lower half of the gateway is of marble. The plan includes a courtyard bordered on either side by an arcade set on columns. The classrooms are domed. The Ak Medrese at Niğde (1409), built by the Karamanlıs, is in good preservation. It is symmetrical, in two storeys, with vaults and domes, and with a courtyard surrounded by piers joined by plain, well-proportioned pointed arches. The arched veranda on the upper floor gives an original appearance to the front on either side of the gateway. Further novelties are the two small ogee arches, with a column in the middle, framed by a large arch. The Vâcîdiye Medrese at Kütahya (1314), a work of the Germiyanlıs, was used as an observatory; an interesting feature is the small round aperture (*opaion*) for observing the stars which is let into the domes of the rooms beside the eyvan.

Ottoman Period. In general, the medreses continue the Seljuk tradition, except that they are mostly single-storeyed with a courtyard. This latter is surrounded by arcades supported on columns; these porticoes, like the students' rooms, are domed. The eyvan is now a closed and domed schoolroom. Buildings with an L- or U-shaped plan are also to be met with. The most important feature of the period is that an assortment of medreses, arranged either haphazard or in geometrical groups, collect around the mosque to form a University City. Other signs of a new style are the abandonment of the exaggerated decoration of the Seljuk gateways, the stone or stone-and-brick façade with double row of windows, and the roofing with lead-covered domes. As in the case of other types of building, İznik possesses the earliest Ottoman medrese, that of Süleyman Pasha (1336?), now ruined. It has a U-shaped plan, with many domes; the large dome over the closed schoolroom rests on pendentives. In the early Bursa period it was usual, as in the Murad Hüdavendigâr, for the functions of mosque and medrese to be combined. The earliest medrese at Bursa is that of Yıldırım (1394): its Şifaiye is also the first Ottoman mental hospital. The plans of the two buildings are almost identical. The Şifaiye is oblong in form, comprising a long courtyard surrounded by a columned arcade, with rooms clustered around it. The porticoes are equipped with steps, necessitated by the slope on which the building stands; this is also the reason why the gate is not aligned with the schoolroom—architecturally an important point. Inside and outside, the patterned facing of the stone-and-brick walls

83

18
87

15a

15c

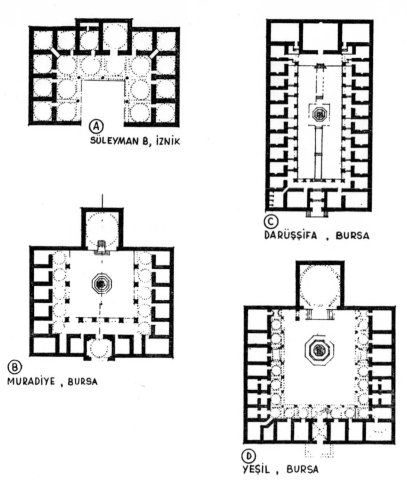

15. *Sketch plans of Ottoman medreses*

gives an effect of colour; the roof, and the dome of the schoolroom, are covered with tiles.

15d   The Green Medrese (1421) is now a museum. Its square schoolroom forms a projection, the model for which was supplied by the medrese of **16** Çelebi Mehmet at Merzifon (1414), though in the latter case there are four projections, each with a single domed room. Architecturally this is connected with the Seljuk type comprising four eyvans. The medrese **15b, 84** of Murad II (1447) has been restored and turned into a dispensary.

    At Edirne, the second Ottoman capital, we have the medical school of **17, 85** Beyazıt II. This is of normal U-shape; but the mental hospital beside it is quite original. For the mental patients there are separate rooms,

38

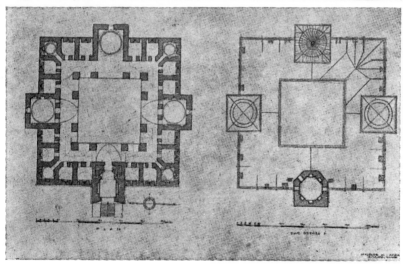

16. *Plan and perspective of Çelebi Mehmet Medrese, Merzifon*

39

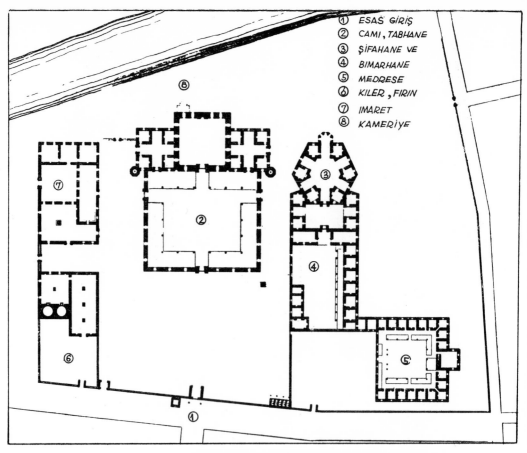

*17. General plan of Mental Hospital (şifaiye) and Medical School
(Tip Medresesi), Edirne*

while for the psychopathical cases there is a communal hall of hexagonal
shape, with dome open to the sky and a water-basin beneath. At one end
86 of this hall is a dais for musicians; the acoustics are excellent. This
building may be considered a monument not only to Ottoman medicine
but also to Ottoman civilization; in Europe at this period lunatics were
still regarded as renegades and submitted to torture. At Bursa the
mosque-complexes are haphazard in arrangement, while at Edirne they
are on a partially geometric plan. In contrast, at Istanbul the grouping
9 of medreses around the Fâtih Mosque (1471) is strictly geometrical.
Here we see the first Ottoman university city. It comprises a great
variety of buildings, including 16 medreses, with eight closed and

40

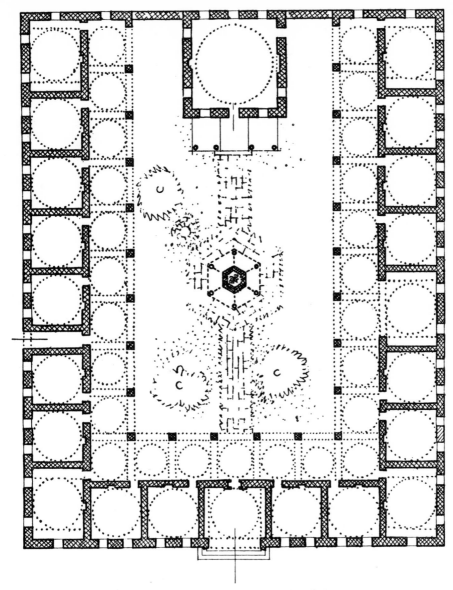

18. Plan of Beyazıt II Medrese, Istanbul

eight open schoolrooms, 230 rooms and 32 lavatories, a school, a library, an asylum, a hospice, a market and private stables. These buildings, together with the mosque in the middle of the great square, form a veritable city of domes. They have now been restored and with the addition of sanitary arrangements are used to-day as a student's

41

home. Upon this admirable plan the Turkish architects of the sixteenth to eighteenth centuries built many similar medreses in various places; among them the Süleymaniye group at Istanbul (1557) is truly a masterpiece.

Mausolea

In the historical section above, mention was made of the origin and architectural connections of the turret-tombs in the great Seljuk cities such as Horasan, Merv and Rey. These are türbes with a high drum and dome, and are called in Turkish, *kümbet*. The Seljuk examples in Persia have a front decorated with fascicles and a pattern of glazed brick.

Anatolian Seljuk and Beylik Periods. This type of building, which the Turks brought to Anatolia, continues the traditional forms, except that stone is used in place of brick and the decoration takes the form of relief. In addition to the rectangle and circle, polygonal shapes are very frequent. These polygons are joined by means of triangular surfaces to a square base resting on the earth. The mummified bodies were

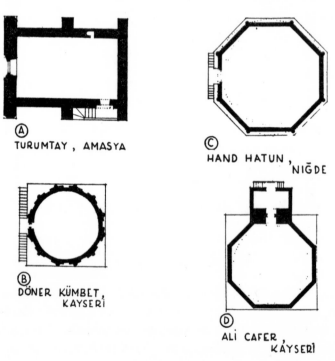

19. *Typical plans of Seljuk türbes*

42

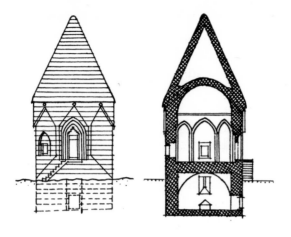

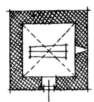
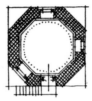

20. Plans, façade and section of Mausoleum
of Melik Gazi, Kırşehir

placed in a crypt. Above this, on the main floor, is a cenotaph and place
of prayer approached by a flight of steps; the roof consists on the
inside of a flat dome and on the outside of a conical structure.

The türbe of Halife Gazi at Amasya (1146) is one of the oldest
monuments in Anatolia. It is a Danişmend building of stone, octagonal
in form, with door and decoration of archaic style. The Turumtay
Türbe (1278) is a Seljuk monument; its oblong plan and gently sloping   19a
roof are original features.

The mausoleum of Melik Gazi at Kırşehir (1250?) is remarkable for   20, 90
the graceful way in which it blends into the ground. With its conical
roof, joined to the octagonal body by triangular surfaces whose ex-
tremities project outwards and downwards like eaves, it has all the
character of a tent in stone.

Kayseri is distinguished also by its mausolea. The richest of them in point of decoration, the Döner Kümbet (1276), is a dodecagonal structure formed of blind arcades. Side by side with geometrical designs we find fanshaped palmettes and birds and lions in relief. The mausoleum of Hudabend Hatun at Niğde (1312), an impressive building, is remarkable for having, among its floral and geometrical ornamentation, reliefs representing birds, stags and animals with human heads. The Sırçalı Kümbet at Kayseri (1349) on the other hand has the form of a plain cylinder. The mausoleum of Ali Cafer, built in the same period, differs from the rest in having a low vestibule at the entrance. That of Hand or Mahperi Hatun (1237), which adjoins the mosque and medrese, belongs to a different category.

The mausoleum of Sheikh Hasan Bey at Sivas (1347), known as the 'Stunted Minaret,' with its cylindrical body of patterned brick, deserves mention as one of the monuments which link Anatolian Seljuk architecture to the Great Seljuk tradition. We must notice also the polygonal mausoleum with pointed conical roof which is attached to the Çifte Minareli Medrese at Erzurum: its blind arcades were copied in the Döner Kümbet at Kayseri. Still earlier, about the end of the twelfth century, a third form of this 'arcaded cylinder' type was originated at Erzurum, as we see in the Triple Mausoleum, a work of the Saltuk period. This very original type is especially common in the Van district; the mausolea at Ahlat, such as that of Emîr Bayındır (1491), with open arcades supported on columns running all round, may be quoted as examples.

Ottoman Period. Certain points of difference from the Seljuk period may be noticed. The sarcophagus and the mescit are located on the same level. The Ottoman buildings have upper and lower windows and columns. They are invariably roofed with a dome. The decoration is restricted to coloured patterns and facing of glazed tile, applied inside instead of outside.

The türbe of Hadji Hamza at İznik (1345), with its conical roof over a rectangular body, shows a continuance of the Seljuk tradition into the Ottoman period. The türbe of Saltuk Dede has a dome resting on four open arches. The double türbe of the family at Çandarlı Hayrüddin Pasha (1378), comprising two adjoining rectangular buildings, is archaic in style; one of its domes is in the form of a skylight.

44

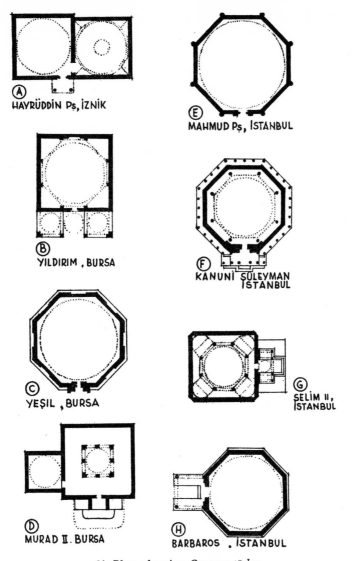

21. Plans of various Ottoman türbes

At Bursa one of the oldest buildings is the türbe of Beyazıt the
Thunderbolt (1406). But a more interesting building is that of Çelebi
Mehmet (1421); its octagonal body was covered, up to the level of the
high drum of the dome, with faience of a dazzling brilliance. The
presence of a crypt and entrance gateway marks a survival of the
Seljuk tradition. The cemetery beside the Muradiye Mosque, containing 11 türbes, is especially remarkable. The türbes are in general four,

21b

21c

93

45

six or eight-sided; the façade is composed of stone and brick arranged
95a in patterns. The interior is richly faced with coloured tiles. The simplest
21d, 94 and most beautiful of them is the türbe of Murad II (1451) rectangular
in plan, it has a dome supported on four piers, with an aperture open
to the sky, permitting the rain and snow to fall upon the tomb.

Nearly all the Ottoman Sultans are buried in Istanbul. One of the
21e oldest türbes is that of Mahmut Pasha, Grand Vizier of Mehmet the
Conqueror (1464). It is octagonal in shape; with its façades of geometrically patterned tiles inlaid into the stone, it is the only building in
Istanbul that recalls the Seljuk style of decoration. The türbe of Hüsrev
Pasha, Vizier of Süleyman the Lawgiver (1545), with its stonework and
dome, is as it were an imitation of the Turkish mausolea in Azerbaijan.
96 The türbe of Şehzade Mehmet (1548) is another octagon; its coloured
stone inlay is reminiscent of the Mameluke buildings in Cairo, while the
sections of the dome adorned with pipe-moulding recall the early
21f Turkish structures. In the türbe of Süleyman the Lawgiver (1566) the
great Sinan, who was partial to ornamentation in this class of building,
has created a masterpiece. The main body of the building rises above a
penthouse supported on columns; with a view to both interior and
exterior effect, the roof is formed of two domes of different curvature,
one within the other. The triple windows are framed in a pointed arch.
By means of these special features the architect has suited the monument to the Sultan's title of 'Magnificent': as if to emphasize this
point, he has built the adjoining türbe of Hurrem Sultan (Roxelane)
in a very simple style (1573). All who are interested in the technique of
21g Turkish faience ornamentaion should visit the türbes of Selim II
(1574) and Murad III (1595). The marble türbe of Sultan Hamid I
(1789) is baroque; that of Sultan Mahmut II (1839) is in Empire
99 style, and that of Fuad Pasha (1868) eclectic. At the same time, in their
plan and structure they preserve the traditional Ottoman forms; the
new style is confined merely to the minor architectural features. The
98 türbes of Mihrişah (1792) and Nakşidil Sultan (1816) are of the Turco-
Baroque style, but cylindrical in form. Of this unusual style the simplest
specimen is the Yeni Türbe (1854?). Finally, the türbe of Sultan
Reşad (1913) is in the neo-classical Ottoman style; this the last of the
Ottoman Sultans' türbes.

*   *   *   *

In medieval Turkey, guest-houses were available for every class of person. The buildings erected to afford a night's lodging to travellers, merchants and postal convoys are called Khans; they are situated in the cities and at intervals of a day's journey on the road. On the caravan routes a more luxurious type was in use, called Caravanserai or Sultan Khan. These caravanserais are the medieval equivalent of the modern 'motel.' Among the Turks, hospitality to strangers is traditional; accordingly, no payment was made for lodging in the caravanserais. There was, however, a charge for the use of khans in the cities, and also for entering and leaving the cities.

Seljuk and Beylik Periods. In the khans and caravanserais the travelling merchant would attend to the safety of his goods and wares, to the repair of his vehicles and the needs of his camels and horses, do his buying and selling, perform his ablutions and devotions and, a day or so later pursue his journey. In time of war these buildings were also used for storing food and munitions. These were the requirements which the architect's plans were devised to meet. As in the Seljuk medreses, a strong gateway was built; this is the only external architectural feature, 100 and all the decoration is concentrated upon it. The gateway leads into a hall with vaults supported on columned arcades and covered with a flat roof. Round this hall are corridors for the tethering of animals, and round these again, at a higher level, are similar corridors with fire place and benches for the men to sleep. In the larger khans, however, the gateway leads into an open courtyard. Around this are arched and vaulted storerooms for baggage, hay and oats, separate private rooms with hearth, dormitories, bathroom and lavatory, as well as the gateway rooms for the inn-keeper and janitor, a coffee-room, repair-shops for the vehicles, a smithy, and stables for the animals. In hot regions a stairway also leads up from one side of the courtyard to the flat roof for the evening assembly. In the caravanserais an additional feature is 23 a small mosque for communal prayer raised on four arches in the middle of the courtyard. From the courtyard a second gateway leads into a covered hall which served as winter quarters; in the middle of this is a dome with an aperture for light and ventilation. The walls of these single-storeyed buildings are of rubble, but the façade, piers and arches are faced with cut stone blocks. The majority were built in the thirteenth

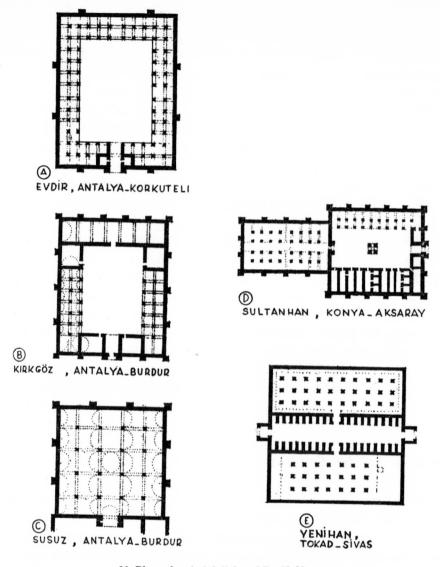

A — EVDIR, ANTALYA-KORKUTELI

B — KIRKGÖZ, ANTALYA-BURDUR

C — SUSUZ, ANTALYA-BURDUR

D — SULTAN HAN, KONYA-AKSARAY

E — YENIHAN, TOKAD-SIVAS

22. *Plans of typical Seljuk and Beylik khans*

century.

The khans of Altınapa (1201) and Kızılören (1204) on the Konya-
22a Beyşehir road are the earliest examples. The Evdir Khan (1210–1219)
on the Anatalya-Korkuteli road has a courtyard and is considered the
22b prototype of the Ottoman khans. The Kırkgöz Khan (1236–1246) on
the road from Anatalya to Burdur has a vaulted roof and an open

courtyard to which a long narrow hall has been added. The Susuz 22c Khan farther north on the same road is of similar date but is of the closed type with vaulted roof. The exterior is fortified with tower-like buttresses. A lantern turret rising in the middle, the decoration of the gateway, and the regular stone masonry, are striking features.

The khan of Ezine Pazar on the Sivas-Amasya road is an oblong structure measuring 37 by 16·50 m.; on either side of the central passage is a raised platform 1·50 m. high where visitors might sit; in the middle of each arch is a hearth; the sloping roof rests on pointed vaults. The caravanserais are, as it were, a souvenir left by the Anatolian Seljuk builders to the world of Turkish Islamic architecture. Even to-day, in the ruins that survive on the now deserted caravan routes, we can perceive the full brilliance and high artistic level of the Seljuk culture. The interior of the Sultan Khan or Palaz Khan on the Kayseri-Sivas road (1236) gives the impression of a fine cathedral; and another impressive example of this type is the Sultan Khan on the Konya-Aksaray 22d road (1229). Both buildings have, in the centre of the courtyard, a 101 mescit approached by steps; its lower part is an empty space surrounded by four open arches. The Sarı Khan near Ürgüp has a similar plan, 23 except that the mescit is over the gateway. The Karatay Khan (1241) on the Kayseri-Malatya road is remarkable for its decoration of human and animal figures: their presence may be attributed to the tradition of totemism and the Uygur animal calendar. Unusual features in the Zazadin Khan near Konya (1236) are its broad courtyard and entrance eccentrically placed, and the conspicuous blue and white stone courses of its gateway.

The Yeni Khan on the Tokad-Sivas road (1317–1335?) is probably of 22e the Beylik period; peculiar features are the rows of shops on either side of a central passage, and the doors at either end. This is really a market-khan, suggestive of the Ottoman markets. The khan of Eşrefoğlu at Bayşehir (1296?) comprises a central hall with two piers and six domes, surrounded on all four sides by shops. This is a market-khan for cotton-thread and textiles.

Ottoman Period. The khans now acquire more of a commercial character; provision is made especially for the collective safety of the merchants' wares and for the practical needs of commercial life. The Ottoman khans consist of rooms arranged around a courtyard behind open

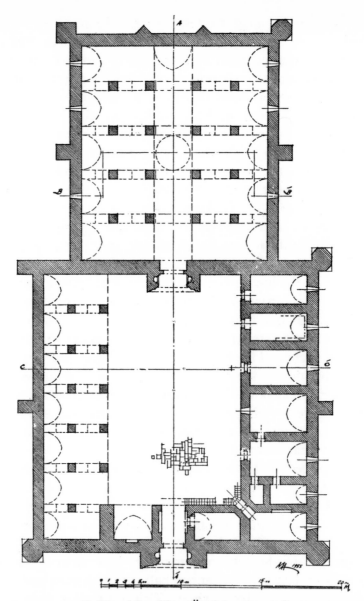

23. Plan of Sarı Khan, Ürgüb (reconstructed)

arcaded galleries. These rooms are well lighted and equipped with hearths and shelves. The sloping roof rests on vaults or domes; both roof and domes are lead-covered. They are built in stone or brick and have generally two storeys, of which the lower is occupied by shops and storerooms, the upper by living-rooms. In the middle of the courtyard

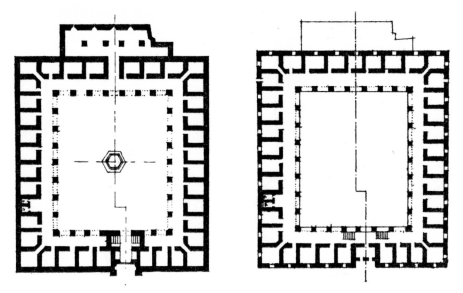

24. Ground and first floor plan of Bey Khan, Bursa, early Ottoman period (reconstructed)

there is usually a mescit set over a water-basin or şadırvan. They follow
the general plan of the Seljuk khans, and were built for preference in the
towns.

At Bursa and Istanbul the khans stood in rows along either side of a
main street, and formed the business quarter of the city. They are,
accordingly, important for the development of Turkish town-planning
just as much as from the architectural point of view.

The khans of Bursa are, in general, rectangular, with plain façade,
and roofed over. The oldest is the Bey Khan, of the time of Orhan
Gazi (1339?), now called the Emîr Khan; but it has lost its original
form. The İpek Khan (silk market), of which little but the shops
remains to-day, was built by Sultan Çelebi Mehmet to provide funds
for the Green Mosque; this was also the purpose of the Geyve Khan,
some of whose rooms, with their iron doors, have preserved their
original form. The Koza Khan (1489) has survived as a place of business
to our own time, and is used to-day as a market. Over a water-basin
in the middle of its interior court it has a domed octagonal mescit:
the dome of the mescit and the roof of the khan are both covered with
lead. Its architect was Pulat Şahoğlu Abdülali. The Pirinç Khan (rice
market), built in 1507, with its double row of saddlers' shops, is a typical
specimen of the market-khan. Once a fine stone building, the work of

24
102

51

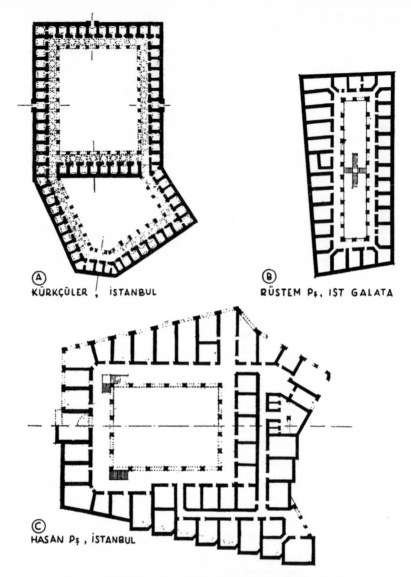

25. *Typical plans of Ottoman khans, Istanbul*

Yakup Şah and Abdullahoğlu Ali, it is to-day in ruins. It had originally 40 rooms on the upper floor and 38 storerooms on the lower; its roof was formerly covered with lead, later replaced by tiles. Both of these khans were built by Beyazıt II to provide funds for his mosque in Istanbul. The Fidan Khan, of khan of Mahmut Pasha, is a stone and brick building; on its upper floor it has 50 rooms, on its lower floor 30 rooms and 18 storerooms. The stables on the east side are now ruined. Over its vaults and domes was an outward-sloping roof covered with lead.

The khans of Istanbul have two or three storeys. In order to avoid having irregularly shaped rooms, due to the winding streets, the façade is interrupted by projections (*cumba*) supported on consoles: in this respect they differ from those of Bursa. Furthermore, the courtyard only rarely contains a waterbasin and mescit. We mention a few characteristic examples.

The Çuhacı Khan (cloth market), of the fifteenth century, is believed to be the oldest in Istanbul. Its courtyard, in two storeys, has arcades with pointed arches; the stone and brick masonry is reminiscent of Bursa. This is one of the 16 khans of the great covered market; these market-khans are more properly regarded as factories.

The Kürkçü Khan (1467?), or fur market, is a work of Mahmut 25a Pasha, and stands at the head of the market of his name. On the outside are low shops; inside are two courtyards, one of which, however, has entirely lost its proper shape. Its great courtyard, measuring 45 by 40 m., is surrounded by galleries in two storeys formed of arcades supported on pillars; behind these there were once 167 rooms. The khan at Bursa built by this same Pasha is less than half this size.

There are two khans bearing the name of Rüstem Pasha (1560?), one on each side of the Golden Horn. That beside the Rüstem Pasha Mosque is in two parts, called the Great and Little Çukur Han; that on the Galata side is known as the Kurşunlu (Leaden) Khan. The latter has pointed arches and cross-vaults of brick; its courtyard, measuring 8·25 by 4·70 m. and surrounded by arcades on stone piers, is in the long axis of the building; from its centre, stairs ascend to the galleries. This plan is highly original and indeed unique. 25b

The Vezir Khan (1647?), of oblong form, is one of the latest works of the classical period. The courtyard is surrounded by arcades in two storeys, whereas the exterior is in three storeys, with shops on the ground-floor. The gateway is arched and is reminiscent of the Sassanid eyvans.

The Büyük Valide Hanı (1650?) is constructed of stone blocks and rubble. It has three courtyards one behind another, in the second of which was a wooden mescit which was burned down some years ago.

53

It has a gallery supported on piers of stone blocks; the gallery and the rooms behind it are roofed with domes.

104 The Simkeşhane (1716) was a khan combining the functions of a silver-thread (*sırma*) factory, market and mint. On two sides of the courtyard, between it and the street, the rooms are arranged on either side of a corridor; this is a departure from the normal plan, by which the rooms are usually placed on one side only of an open gallery around the court. The façades show alternating courses of stone and brick, and the ground-floor was occupied by shops roofed with semi-circular vaults of brick. The front was cut away for road widening in 1956.

The Great Yeni Han was built in 1764: its skilfully designed façades are characteristic. Its two courtyards, and its arcades with their semi-circular brick arches, are in three storeys—a departure from the normal rule. Owing to the steep slope of the street which passes the front the lower side of the khan shows four storeys; on the bottom floor is a row of shops. Beside it stands the Little Yeni Han; this has a mosque set in one corner on the first floor and approached by an exterior staircase.

105 The Fourth Vakıf Hanı (1918) is a shop and office building on an entirely new plan; it is the finest of the khans built by the neo-classic architect Kemal Bey. In the early twentieth century khans were built purely as places of business; the function of providing lodging has in our times been taken over by the hotels.

Covered Markets

The use of khans as markets was mentioned above. Of Turkish market-buildings the outstanding characteristic is that they are covered over. These domed halls, supported internally as a rule by pillars, are called *bedesten*; they formerly served for the sale of silk and other precious fabrics, but nowadays as markets for jewellery and all kinds of valuable goods. The market itself, called *arasta*, consists of shops with vaulted roof or with projecting eaves, arranged on either side of an open or vaulted street. A peculiarity of these markets is that they are always built beside a mosque and were intended to provide a permanent source of revenue for religious charities. Their architectural character is functional and aims at simplicity and strength. The material used is stone and brick with lighting provided by small windows in the façade or in the roof. The shops are from 3 to 5 m. wide, and of similar or rather greater depth.

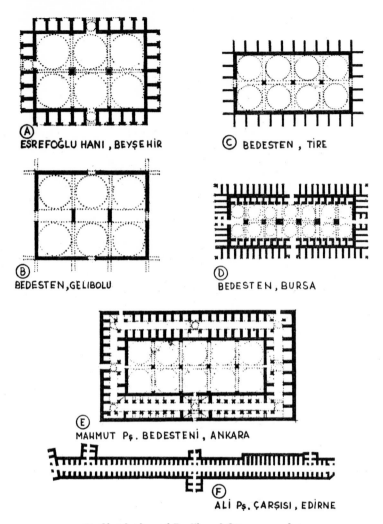

ⒶAȘREFOĞLU HANI , BEYȘEHİR

ⒷBEDESTEN,GELIBOLU

ⒸBEDESTEN , TİRE

ⒹBEDESTEN , BURSA

ⒺMAHMUT Pș. BEDESTENİ , ANKARA

ⒻALİ Pș. ÇARȘISI , EDİRNE

26. Sketch plans of Beylik and Ottoman markets

In the Seljuk period independent market buildings are unknown, and this function was performed by the khans and caravanserais. There is at Alâiye (Alanya) a building with shops over a courtyard and a covered hall at one end; it is doubtful whether this should be regarded as a khan or a bedesten. Its date is likewise uncertain. Riefstahl believes it to be an Ottoman structure. On the other hand, the khan of Eşrefoğlu at Beyşehir, **26a** a building of the Beylik period, with its exterior shops, is of bedesten type. Its plan, including six domes and two piers, is indeed identical with that of the (sixteenth century?) bedesten at Gelibolu, except that **26b**

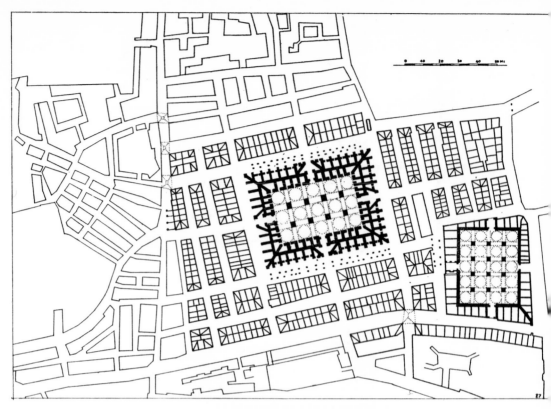

27. Great Covered Market at Istanbul, general plan

in the latter case the exterior shops are lacking. The covered market at Tire (1397?) has three piers and eight domes; there are no shops on the outside. That at Edirne (1418) has six piers and 14 domes, with exterior shops. Similar to this last is the bedesten at Bursa (1405?) where the stone and brick masonry of the inner walls produces a colourful interior. A further feature common to both is the possession of a treasury. The present Hittite Museum at Ankara was formerly the bedesten of Mahmut Pasha (1465); its plan, with 10 domes supported on a single row of four pillars, follows that at Tire. These are all developments of one and the same plan.

    The market of Ali Pasha at Edirne (1569) was built by the great Sinan. It is a handsome building of arasta type, 300 m. long, with six gates. The arasta of Selimiye (late sixteenth century), a work of Davut Ağa, approximates to Sinan's designs; while the market of Niğde

26c

26d

106, 26e

26f

56

(seventeenth century) is also of arasta type, but is only a modest country-town market.

In Istanbul, the market built by Mehmet the Conqueror has 15 domes and two rows of four pillars; its plan and structure follow the bedesten tradition of Bursa and Edirne. Süleyman the Magnificent also built a market of similar type with 20 domes; its plan is identical with that of the Ulu Cami at Bursa. The regular courses of plain brick produce a colourful interior, though lacking in decoration. These two buildings, with the addition from time to time of streets and arasta-type markets, comprise the famous Covered Market of Istanbul with 27 all its fairy-tale glamour. It is a veritable market-city, covering 30,700 sq. m., and including 65 streets, a square, 3,000 shops, 1,000 rooms, 18 gates, eight fountains, five mosques and mescits, a school, wells and running water, and two fire-pumps; around it are 16 large khans. These are its extant features; formerly it was still larger and its contents more varied; at night its gates were closed and guarded by hundreds of watchmen. In the time of the Sultans Mehmet and Süleyman the market was of wood; following a fire it was rebuilt in its present form in 1701. Subsequently it suffered from numerous other fires. The latest of these, on November 26th, 1954, destroyed more than three-fifths of the building. The work of restoration was at once begun, and a part of the market was reopened in 1956. Each street is devoted to a particular branch of commerce. The khans have two or three storeys, the market itself only one. An important peculiarity is that the building is cool in summer and warm in winter. This great covered market is of immense interest; but architecturally the 'Egyptian' Market of Istanbul (1660) is un- 107, 108 deniably superior.

There are many markets in Istanbul and in other Turkish cities; the largest of these, after that in Istabul, is the Covered Market at Kayseri.

Palaces and Houses

The Horasan house-plan, with courtyard and four eyvans, of which the caravanserais and medreses were an adaptation, served also as the prototype for the pavilions and main buildings of the palaces. This is borne out by the plan of the Gazne palaces of the eleventh century, which are reckoned among the earliest Turkish works of this kind. The ruins of a palace of this type have recently (1949) been brought to light at Leşker-i-Pazar. The palaces at Samarra, in point of design and

57

situation, show distinct resemblances to the Gazne palaces; and it is understandable that the Seljuks too, who were close akin to the Gaznelis, should adopt the same plans. In general, at all periods, the Turkish palace (*saray*) consists of a number of pavilions (*köşk*) and groups of buildings set among a succession of courtyards and gardens with ponds, the whole surrounded by a wall.

Like the palaces of China, these are designed to suit the Turkish climate and way of life. The use of separate palaces for summer and winter reflects the age-old custom of changing residence according to the season. The castles (*kasr*) built in the country on the mountain-tops and frontiers have the form of a fortified château. These palaces, which served both as residences and as seats of government, are built generally of wood and baked or sundried brick; only in the later periods are they of stone.

Anatolian Seljuk Period. By reason of the building materials used, no complete palace of this period has survived to the present day. Of those at Alâiye and Sivas we know no more than their names in ancient texts. On the hill of Alâüddin at Konya one eyvan of the palace of Kılıçarslan II was standing until 50 years ago, but is now destroyed. It is however possible, from old pictures, to obtain some idea of the design and architecture of this building. The palace comprised a number of arched pavilions of brick set on a high platform; the eyvans carried on their outer face small balconies (*cumba*) supported on stepped consoles; the

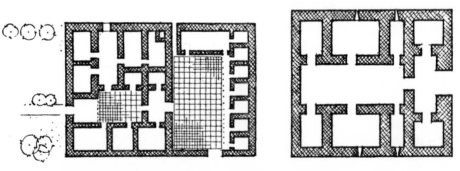

28. *Kubâd-âbâd at Beyşehir, Seljuk period. Plans of reconstruction of main buildings*

walls were faced with tiles. Here we see a clear continuation of the Gazne tradition. In 1949, at Beyşehir near Konya, the ruins of the palace of Alâüddin Keykûbâd were brought to light. Here was the city-centre of Kubâd-âbâd (1227–1235). There still survive some remains of the rubble walls of a small palace on the hilltop and a larger one below. The tiles which cover the walls of the hall resemble in their form, colour and figured designs those of the pavilion on the hill of Alâüddin. The ruins give a good idea of Seljuk building style and material.

In the neighbourhood of Kayseri are the ruins of a palace, the Kubâdiye, and two pavilions that belonged to wealthy Seljuks. Of these last, the pavilion of Haydar Bey is of uncertain date, that of Hızır İlyas dates from 1241; both are of military and monumental character, constructed of brick and stone blocks. The marble gateway of the latter resembles that of other Seljuk buildings. Though they cannot rank as palaces, these pavilions are important specimens of Seljuk civil architecture.

Ottoman Period. The earliest Ottoman palace was built at Bursa by Orhan Bey, conqueror of that city; it was called Bey Sarayı, but nothing remains of it to-day. Of the early Ottoman palaces at Edirne only a few fragmentary ruins are preserved.

At Istanbul the first palace was built by Mehmet the Conqueror in 1454–1458. It was called the Old Palace and stood on the spot now occupied by the University; being made of wood it was destroyed by fire. The Çinili Köşk (1472) on the other hand, also built by Mehmet, 29, 110 is in stone and is still standing complete. It is two storeys and incorporates in its plan the small court with four eyvans seen in the Gazne palaces, but here this court has been roofed over with a dome and made the centre of the building. As in the Seljuk caravanserais and medreses, and in the early Bursa mosques, the rooms are roofed with a dome and a half-dome. The form of the building is the same as in the mosques of Yahşi Bey at Tire and Beylerbeyi at Edirne. The triangular-ribbed vaulting is hidden under the roof-terrace; from outside only the central dome, rising on a drum, is visible. The arch over the eyvan by which the pavilion is entered is faced with mosaic tiles. The general character of the building is wholly in the tradition of the Seljuks of Horasan. This pavilion, together with others scattered at random among the gardens, made up the New Palace of Mehmet the Conqueror (1475–1478).

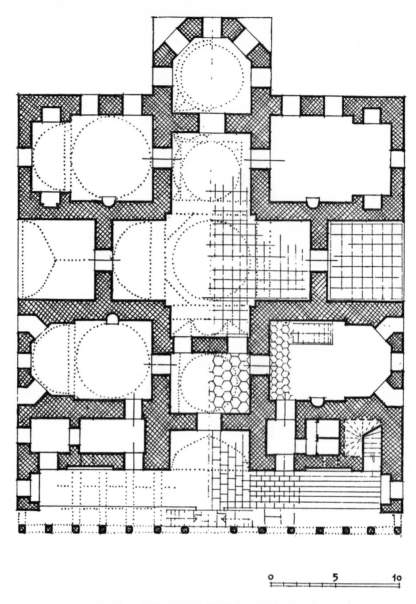

29. Plan of Çinili Köşk (Teiled pavilion), Istanbul

30   The complex known to-day as the Topkapı Palace (Seraglio) grew out of the various additions to the New Palace made by the Sultans through the centuries. From the fifteenth century until they moved to the palaces on the Bosporus in the nineteenth, this was the residence of the Ottoman

60

Sultans. But it was not only a residence; it served at the same time as a centre of government and of culture. Since the establishment of the Republic in 1925 it has been a museum open to the public. Nowhere else is it possible to find an assemblage of buildings which affords such an opportunity to study in one place almost the entire history of the Ottoman Empire and all its architectural periods. Originally comprising 348 rooms and covering 699,000 sq. m., the palace has in the course of time lost many of its pavilions, particularly those near the shore. With its buildings and annexes set among green gardens, it may truly be called a small city, comprising as it does five groups of apartments, two groups of offices, eight servants' quarters, 10 mosques, 14 baths, two hospitals, five schools, 12 libraries, 22 fountains, a fishpond and vineyard, four inner and one outer court, the whole enclosed on the land side by a wall. The outer or fifth court has now been converted into a park of European character (Gülhane Park): formerly it served the palace as a hunting and sports ground, and included flower, fruit and vegetable gardens. The first court has also been modernized, but the others and especially the second, have kept their character as Turkish gardens asymmetrically arranged with lawns, flower beds, nurseries, upright trees lining the paths, and water in appropriate places. It is a praiseworthy fact that this layout corresponds to the modern conception of landscape gardening. Indeed, the whole arrangement of the palace, with its ungeometrical sub-divisions and its terrace walls counteracting the steep slope of the ground, conforms admirably to present-day principles of town planning.

The entrance gate to the second court resembles the city gates of Western Asia. This court served as a place of assembly and for public service. Accordingly it provided the scene of Councils of State and Assemblies (*Kubbe altı*), and contains the kitchens where food was cooked for the 5,000 occupants of the palace. The court is surrounded by a portico with arcades. At the far end, in front of the gate giving access to the third court, is a porch (*sayvan*) with very wide eaves; here the throne was placed, and here the coronation ceremony was performed, greetings were paid to the sultan on the occasion of religious holidays, and sessions were held for the presentation of petitions and complaints (*ayak divanı*). This part of the palace corresponds to the camp outside the sultan's tent in time of war. Between this court and the third, or *Enderun,* are the women's quarters. The harem consists of

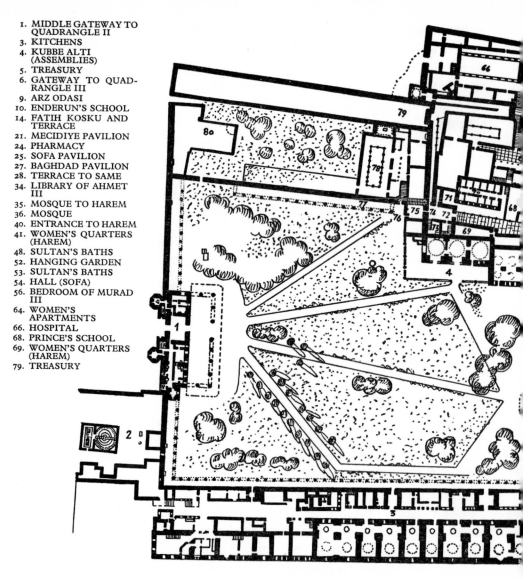

30. Topkapı Pale

irregular groups of buildings set around small courtyards; owing to the
slope of the ground it is partly in two storeys. The separate quarters for
the Great Sultan, the minor sultans, the royal princes, the concubines
and the black eunuchs are of individual interest. With its sitting-
rooms and dining-rooms, baths, mosque, school, eunuch's dormitories
and servants' quarters, this section of the palace is like an independent

62

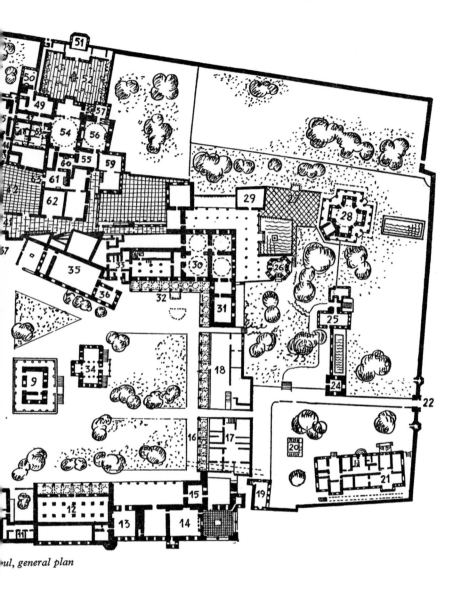

ul, general plan

parish. As in Turkish private houses, in contrast to the plainness of the exterior architecture, the interior of the harem is richly decorated in the style of various periods.

In the third court the Conqueror's Suite is of interest; the building in which envoys were received by the sultan (*arz odası*) is a marvel of fifteenth-century Turkish civil architecture. Among the other buildings, the library of Sultan Ahmet (1719) is remarkable for its plan and its marble façade.

For the history of architecture, however, the most interesting buildings, in the writer's opinion, are in the fourth court.

112, 113   The Baghdad Pavilion (1638), with its four eyvans and central dome, recalls the plan of the Çinili Köşk. Its terraces, with views embracing the Bosporus and Golden Horn, are surmounted by a wide-eaved roof supported on arcades. The walls are faced, inside and out, with tiles. Pure Turkish building tradition, dating back into Central Asiatic times, finds its fullest expression in this masterpiece of classical Ottoman architecture.

The Revan Pavilion (1635) is of similar character. Both these buildings are constructed of stone and brick and set upon a high podium.

114   The Sofa Pavilion, or Pavilion of Mustafa Pasha (1704), is built on a terrace almost in the centre of the fourth court. It is in Rococo-Turkish style. Built of wood as a summer pavilion, very light and airy, almost diaphanous, it answers perfectly to modern architectural conceptions. Beside it is a service building constructed partly of stone.

The Mecidiye Pavilion (1840 ?) is on a terrace overlooking the Sea of Marmara. It is built in a European style totally foreign to Turkish architecture. This is the last pavilion in the fourth court, and with it the Topkapı Palace comes to an end.

31   The palace of İbrahim Pasha (fifteenth century ?), overlooking the park opposite St. Sophia, is a private vizier's palace standing in a single block. It has three storeys and measures 142 by 75 m., with ground floor based upon four courtyards. The upper floor contains 65 rooms and five halls.

The Pavilion of Siyavuş Pasha (1582–1592) is next to the Bahçeli Evler quarter of Istanbul. This too was a vizier's palace, but only a pavilion remains, set on stone pillars and arches over the centre of a swimming pool. Both its form and its architectural detail are highly original.

116   The Palace beside the barracks of Davut Pasha (1603–1615) is an imperial villa, from which Sultan Ahmet I set out to war or on hunting excursions. It is built of stone in two storeys, with arches and dome, and is one of the latest and finest specimens of classical Turkish architecture.

The castle of İshak Pasha (1785) is a fortified Turkish Château at

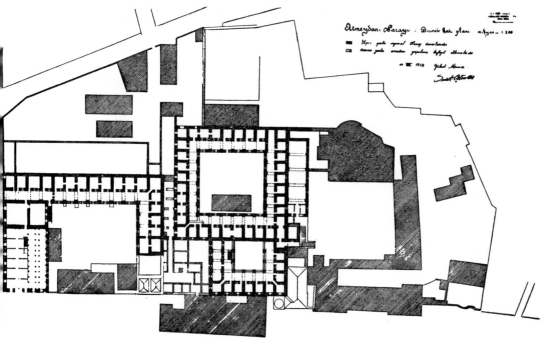

31. Palace of Ibrahim Pasha at Istanbul, restored plan

Doğu Beyazıt on the borders of Turkey and Persia. It is a vast structure of stone, built as a citadel on a high hill. Its plan is based on four courtyards containing men's, women's and servants' quarters, a ceremonial suite, and various appendages. Among these a bathing establishment, mosque and mausoleum, vineyards attached to the harem, and halls lighted from above, are deserving of notice.

The Pavilion of Aynalı Kavak on the Golden Horn is a comparatively **117** modern pavilion (1791) replacing a part of the old palace of the same name; it was formerly known as the Hasbahçe Pavilion. It is in two storeys, half of wood and half of stone. The architectural detail is Turco-Baroque, but the plan, the order of the façade, and the overhanging roof are in the classical Turkish style.

Of the palaces on the Bosporus many have been destroyed. Some of these have been replaced by modern tall buildings.

Dolmabahçe Palace was rebuilt by Abdülmecit in 1853. Despite its **118** Baroque-Empire style, it nevertheless shows here and there—as in the detail and plan—traces of Turkish tradition. Its plan is due to the architect Hacı Emin Pasha, its style and construction to the builder

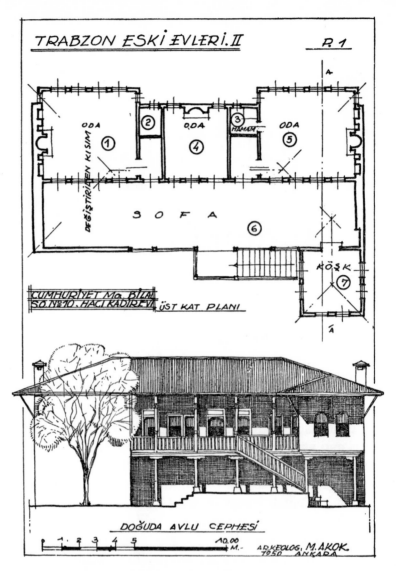

32a. An old Turkish house at Trabzon: first floor plan, and elevation

Karabet Balyan. The same observations apply also to the Beylerbeyi Palace (1865).

The Çiragan Palace at Beşiktaş (1871) is now a burnt-out ruin. Its plan and structure are Turkish, but the style is Eclectic.

Yıldız Palace was from 1808–1908 the last residence of the Ottoman Sultans. It comprises a complex of numerous pavilions, which, for all

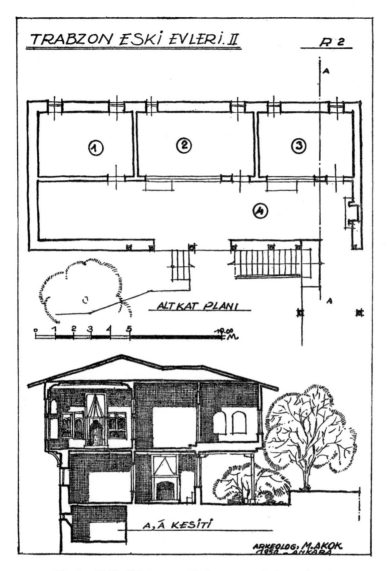

TRABZON ESKİ EVLERİ. II

R 2

① ② ③

④

ALT KAT PLANI

0 1 2 3 4 5

-10.00
E.M.

A,Ā KESİTİ

ARKEOLOG: M.AKOK
1950 - ANKARA

32b. An old Turkish house at Trabzon: ground plan and section

their hybrid style, by their situation in an extensive garden recall the old Turkish town-planning as we see it in the Topkapı Palace.

Old Turkish Houses. Being for the most part light structures of wood **32a, b** and dried brick, none of these survived more than 100 years. Turkey includes regions varying greatly both in climate and in their natural

67

features, and house-types vary accordingly in plan and in material. In the east, for example, the houses are of stone, with few windows, whereas in hot regions they have eyvans, ponds and tree-shaded courts. Such, for instance, are the houses of Diyarbakır, built on the plan of those at Horasan. In temperate regions, on the other hand, the kernel of the plan is a covered hall, and in seaside towns the houses have many windows. The most highly developed and classic types are to be seen in the cities of Bursa and Istanbul. We can do no more, in this concise survey, than to indicate the general character and common features shared by all Turkish houses. The following terms are used for the various kinds of private residence: for small and plain town-dwellings, *house*; for larger and richer houses, *konak*; for those by the seashore, *yalı*; and for those set in summer gardens, *köşk*.

All houses are divided into two parts, the men's quarters (*selâmlık*) and the women's quarters (*harem*): in the larger houses these two parts are entirely separate. The gate of the selâmlık leads into a large garden-court in one corner of which are the kitchen and laundry, each a separate building. Separate again is the bath house. In smaller houses these are included in the main building. The harem has its own private gate, paved court and staircase. On the ground-floor are the servants' rooms. In the Anatolian cities, on the other hand, the house is supported on pillars over an open space serving for coach house, hay-loft and the like, and the staircase leads up from the open court to a room open on one side. On the first floor are the master's and mistress's sitting rooms and reception rooms set end to end around a central hall. Hall and rooms are all similarly equipped. Across the width of the windows is a divan or window-seat, 0·35 m. high and 0·75 m. deep, on which are strewn cushions and pillows; in the middle of the room are more cushions and a charcoal stove. Stools and armchairs date to more recent times. Round the room are alcoves and built-in cupboards.

The interior is light and colourful, great importance being attached to these qualities. Windows are in two rows, an upper and a lower; the lower row provided with lattices, making it impossible to see in from outside when they are opened; alternatively, shutters or venetian blinds are fitted. The upper windows do not open; they have stained glass panes and plaster decoration. The wooden ceilings are adorned with geometrical designs and star-patterns made of thin strips of wood and coloured to resemble the sky on a starry night. The ceilings of houses at Ankara, Bursa and Istanbul in particular would alone afford material for a book. In the Baroque period Renaissance motifs replace the original designs; among them small landscape paintings are to be seen.

Externally the houses are generally of two or three storeys. The 119 ground floor, wholly or partly of stone, is plain and solid. If there is an entresol, it is distinguished by small windows, but does not project beyond the ground floor. The other floors project each beyond the one below. The projections (cumba) are in the shape either of consoles formed of small rafter-ends, as at Ankara, or of curved wooden struts, as in the houses of Bursa and Istanbul. These projections increase the area of the house and at the same time protect the walls of the lower storeys from sun and rain. With the same object, the eaves of the roof are made to project strongly. The external architecture is plain and unadorned, except that in the stone houses of eastern Anatolia, while the exterior façade is still plain, the sides of the courtyard are remarkable for their arched and ornamental masonry. On the shores of the Bosporus in former times the gaily painted yalıs overhanging the sea, with their 122 reflections in the water, used to present a most picturesque appearance; unfortunately, all but one or two of them are now destroyed.

Of the Emirgân yalısı (1640 ?) the harem is gone, but the selâmlık, on 121 two storeys, remains. The ground floor, which is now on the street, was formerly over the sea and was used as a boat-house. The upper floor comprises a group of rooms around a hall with eyvans and a water-basin, and overlooks on the one side the sea and the other a most attractive garden.

The yalı of Hüseyin Pasha at Kanlıca (1698), called also by reason of 120 its colour the Red Yalı, survives in part, raised on pillars over the water. Its plan, and its external and internal architecture, make it a most original seaside residence. The colourful interior decoration is especially attractive. This is the latest example of the classical Turkish style in civil architecture.

Public Baths, Water Installations, Fountains, etc.
Public Baths. Public baths are institutions for the promotion of health and cleanliness; in the seventeenth century there were in Istanbul alone more than 300 of these.

The earliest Moslem baths are in Syria, where it may be thought that the Roman Thermae afforded the model. However, while the Roman and

Byzantine baths were used as places of entertainment, at Damascus they were purely sanitary in purpose. Nor have they any connection with the thermae in point of plan or architecture. The Seljuk baths differ from those of Damascus in having a plan centred on an octagon with four eyvans, and the washing arrangements do not include a pool. The ruins of a bath of this type survive at Nigâr, south of Kirman (see Schroeder, *The Seljuq Period*). In the baths of North Africa bathing begins in the pool; in the Turkish baths there is no such pool, as water which has touched other bodies than one's own is considered used and so unclean. Among the Turks such pools are only used in the thermal baths (*kaplıca*), and then only for medicinal purposes. All that the Romans have bequeathed to the Turkish baths is the heating arrangements and hypocaust technique.

Anatolian Seljuk and Beylik Periods. The Sultan Hamamı at Konya, opposite the mosque of Sahib Atâ, gives a good idea of a Seljuk baths. There are separate twin buildings for men and women: baths of this type are called 'double baths.' The first room to be entered is the disrobing room (*câmegâh*), with marble floor and a fountain in the middle. From here a passage leads to the tepidarium (*soğukluk*), which is used for repose, massage, and for accustoming the body to the heat. After this comes the hot room (*sıcaklık*). This is a domed octagonal hall round which are recesses (eyvan) containing water-basins and private rooms (*halvet*).

The kaplıca at Ilgın (1236) is an early Seljuk work, but its architectural character has been spoilt by subsequent additions.

The baths of Âbid Çelebi (1283–1338), also called the Şifa or Türbe Hamamı, is among the charitable foundations of the Mevlana family. It is of the Karamanoğlu period, and has stone rubble walls, with dome and vaults of brick. The building as a whole, with its centralized plan, is modelled on the Yağı Basan Hamamı at Niksar, a work of the Danişmendli period.

33a   The Meram Hamamı (1423) is one of the 14 baths at Konya. It is a double baths, and is the only inscribed Karamanlı building still standing. Its plan is centralized, symmetrical and rectangular.

Ottoman Period. The baths of the earlier period were taken as a model, developed and brought to perfection. The earliest examples of this

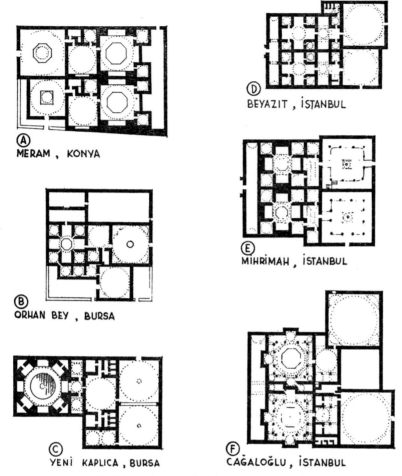

A MERAM , KONYA

B ORHAN BEY , BURSA

C YENİ KAPLICA , BURSA

D BEYAZIT , İSTANBUL

E MİHRİMAH , İSTANBUL

F CAĞALOĞLU , İSTANBUL

33. Plans of various Seljuk and Ottoman baths

period are at Bursa; this city, with its abundant hot springs, also possesses the most important thermal baths.

The baths of Orhan Bey (1339?), beside the Koza Khan, is to-day 33b used as a covered market. It has been burnt down and repaired again and again. It has no inscription, but is believed to have been built together with the mosque of Orhan Bey. In plan it is a double baths, and a surprising feature is the door joining the men's and women's sections.

The old Yeni Hamam (1336?) is the first of the two baths built at Bursa by Orhan the Conqueror. Its present condition is due to much alteration, but if it were excavated and restored we should have one of the very earliest Ottoman baths.

71

The Eski Kaplıca (1389?–1511) shows two building periods. The first dates to the time of Murad I, and comprises the original square plan including the tepidarium and hot room. Its arcades form an octagon on which the domes rest. The columns of these arcades have Byzantine capitals so inappropriate and inconsistent with the rest of the building that it is clear they must have been brought from elsewhere and re-used in this Turkish structure. The general plan of this early part resembles that of the mosque of Orhan and the other mosques in Bursa, except that in order to conserve the heat it is much less lofty. The bather first enters a circular pool 7·30 m. in diameter and 1·30 m. deep, filled from the natural hot springs; he then pours over himself water from taps and basins and makes his way out. In the second period certain additions were made; we learn from the inscription that these are a charitable foundation of Beyazıt II. They comprise on the ground floor a stable, a cookshop and other shops for vendors of soft drinks and bath towels, and on the upper floor a large disrobing room. The architect applied here the combination of dome and half-dome that he had already used in the Beyazıt Mosque in Istanbul. These baths were a social as well as a medical institution, and bathing and service were free of charge. The architecture has undergone so much alteration and modification that it has now lost its meaning; in its present state the domes are covered by a roof of brick tiles.

33c The Yeni Kaplıca (1520–1566) was built by Rüstem Pasha. Here the hot room is an octagon formed by eyvans, and the domes include lighting apertures of special construction. In respect of comfort and general arrangement, and the internal and external space-proportions, this is the finest building of its class.

In Istanbul the architecture of the baths takes a classical form.

The baths of Mahmut Pasha (1466) are the oldest baths surviving in Istanbul, all the others having been burnt down. It is remarkable for its axial plan and highly harmonious architecture. It is still used for its original purpose.

33d The Beyazıt Hamamı (1501) is a double baths built together with the Beyazıt Mosque. Its highly perfected and classicised plan was later adopted by the great Sinan and repeated identically in such of his works 33e as the Çinili Hamam (1546) and the Mihrimah Hamamı (1548).

34, 124 The Haseki Hamamı (1556) is at the end of the park in front of St. Sophia. It is a double baths, symmetrically designed about the longi-

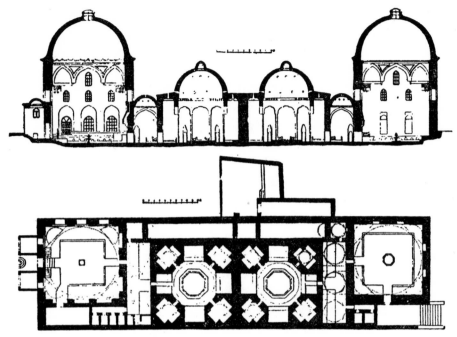

34. Plan and section of Haseki Hurrem Hamamı, Istanbul

tudinal axis. The originality of its plan, its technique and decoration, and the combination of harmonious proportions emphazising the character of the separate parts both inside and out, combine to make this a masterpiece of its kind.

The Cagaloğlu Hamamı (1742) combines the classic type with that of 33f the Eski Kaplıca at Bursa. Its architectural features show a Baroque tendency.

Water Installations, Fountains. In the Moslem religion great value is attached to water. Among the Turks in particular water is important not only for religious and ablutionary purposes, but also in city and social life, in art and architecture. Through some Anatolian houses water runs in an open channel like a small river. At Diyarbakır the ponds in the court-yards of the houses are at the same time refreshing and aesthetically attractive. Similarly ponds with fountains were set in the halls of the houses at Bursa and the yalıs at Istanbul. There is an interesting pond of this kind in the Karatay Medrese at Konya, in the paved floor under the dome; the water ran splashing down a narrow winding

73

F

channel, while the students rested and refreshed themselves beside the pool. There is a similar arrangement in the reception hall of the Gazne palace at Leşker-i-Pazar. In the Blue Medrese at Sivas the pond in the courtyard and the fountain in the façade (which has been flowing for 700 years) are no less artistic and impressive than the medrese itself. In the entrance front of the Sahib Atâ Mosque at Konya there are two public fountains; architecturally they resemble small gateways. The fountains in the ponds inside the Ulu Cami and Green Mosque at Bursa and the Selimiye Mosque at Edirne are still playing to-day. In the hall of the hospital built by Beyazıt at Edirne the sound of the fountain blended with the sounds of music to assist the cure of mental disorders.

Reservoirs and Aqueducts. The Byzantine aqueducts and cisterns at Fâtih being no longer serviceable, the Turks were obliged to instal a new water system for Istanbul. In the time of the great Sinan a network feeding 40 public fountains, now abandoned, supplied the city with water from the Belgrade Forest. The water was collected by means of dams and stored in reservoirs, then conducted down the valleys on arched aqueducts. One of these, the Uzun Kemer, is a stone erection 716 m. long and 26 m. high, of rustic masonry with 50 arches; in it, and especially in the Moğul Ağa arch, we may see how the ancient Roman model has been accommodated to the character of Turkish architecture. On the level ground the water was carried underground through arched tunnels of stone, collected at Eğri Kapı and filtered through water-towers before being distributed to the city.

Public Fountains. The importance attached to these is shown by the fact that in the eighteenth century there were no fewer than 10,390 of them in Istanbul. To-day water is supplied to the houses by modern methods, and these have gradually lost their usefulness. As among the Anatolian Seljuks, they are constructed of stone in the form of an arched door or gateway; the façade has sculptured decoration showing geometrical patterns, plants, flowers and ornamental script. These, with their varied colours—gold, blue, brownish-green and red—make an artistic contrast to the white marble façade. In the country, the fountains set by the roadside at intervals of one hour's journey for the convenience of travellers and caravans, are plain and without decoration; close beside

74

the fountain is a trough for the use of animals, and a group of trees provide a shady resting-place.

In the cities, as a general rule, the fountains have a single façade and are set in the face of a wall or in the ground floor of a building; behind them are water-magazines. A good specimen of this type of public fountain may be seen to-day beside the Galata Tower. This little monument, known as the Bereketzade Fountain, goes back originally to the time of Mehmet the Conqueror, but in its present form it is later (1732). There are also private fountains of this type: characteristic examples, in classic and Baroque style, may be found in the rooms and gardens of the palaces, and in the gardens of the konaks and yalıs. In some cases they have the form of cascades. The principal monumental fountains serve as ornaments in the open spaces, and take the form of solid towers with four faces. One of these is the fountain of Sultan Ahmet **126** III (1728) in front of the Topkapı Palace; the last verse of its dating inscription was composed and written by the Sultan himself. It is a striking work of art, with its wide-eaved, highly wrought roof and decorative workmanship; but if the truth must be told, its design shows that the classical Ottoman architecture had already entered its period of decadence.

The Tophane Fountain (1732) is another monument of this kind. In its decoration, among classical Turkish motifs, stylized dishes of fruit and flower vases strike the eye. Its wide projecting roof, designed both to afford shade and to protect the coloured decoration, was destroyed, but at the time of writing (1957) is being restored.

These buildings, and especially the fountain (1792) in the court of the Süleymaniye Mosque with its pyramid roof, recall the towers of the Horasan Seljuks; thus we see the tradition of Turkish architectural form surviving over almost 1,000 years. Similarly the fountain of Emin Ağa at Dolmabahçe (1740), in the decorative detail of its arches, columns and capitals, despite a certain Rococo tendency characteristic of the period, preserves the same tradition.

The fountain of Hekimoğlu Ali Pasha (1732), though built in the same Baroque period, remains wholly true to the classical Turkish style. It was after this date that French influence, due to historical and political connections, made itself widely felt in Turkish architecture. The Lâleli (1763) and Hamidiye (1777) fountains (*sebili*) are characteristic **128** works of this last period.

At these public fountains (*sebil*) water was served free of charge to all comers. Furthermore, at the time of their first opening fruit drinks (*şerbet*) were distributed for weeks on end, and this gratuity was repeated during the holy months. In plan they comprise a six-, eight-, twelve- or sixteen-sided, or sometimes circular, service hall for the distribution of water, to which another room is sometimes added. In some cases there is also an open fountain in association. The walls are veneered from top to bottom, inside and out, with marble. The spaces between the columns and arches are completely filled by highly artistic bronze railings; on all faces are coloured friezes elegantly inscribed with lines of poetry and verses from the Koran relating to water. These fountains are so situated as to form a private nook or recess set back from the street. In effect these artistic monuments, quite apart from their architectural aspect, have a place in the history of town planning, social charity, stone and metal handiwork, poetry and literature.

Şadırvans. A *şadırvan* is a kind of fountain for washing and ritual ablution in the court of a mosque or medrese. Essentially it comprises an open or covered water-basin with fountain, and taps all round from which water may be drawn. Stone seats and clothes-hooks are provided. **129, 18** The şadırvan of the Beyazıt Medrese is surrounded by columned arcades and covered over by a domed roof with wide eaves. Architecturally the most graceful specimen of this type is the şadırvan in the courtyard of St. Sophia (1740); but that of the Fâtih Mosque, with its conical roof and the upright trees around it, recalling the building tradition of the **54** Seljuk courtyard, is more characteristic. It is also one of the earliest.

Bridges

Here we shall do no more than notice briefly the influence exerted by classical Turkish art and the works of that most prolific of bridge-builders, the great Sinan. Turkish bridges are stone structures with pointed arch, in the Seljuk tradition. But in Sinan's sixteenth century bridges the proportions of the arch are adapted to the power of resistance in the stone, adjustments are made to suit the nature of the ground and the normal and flood levels of the river, the points of abutment are carefully selected, and the central piers are shaped according to their situation. The portative or weight-bearing parts are left unadorned; decoration being confined to the parapet and the stone carrying the inscription. In Sinan's bridges, which have now survived for 400 years, endurance and utility are combined with beauty. The finest is that at Büyük Çekmece, 635 m. long with four arches; while the noble and impressive architecture of the Sinanlı Bridge at Alpullu inspires feelings of admiration no less profound than does his own Süleymaniye Mosque.

CHAPTER THREE

MATERIALS AND CONSTRUCTION

One of the obvious axioms taught by the history of world architecture, is that every nation must build with the materials available in the country in which it lives. Another is that architectural forms, building style, workmanship and art of each nation are affected by those of ruling nations, neighbouring nations and earlier local civilizations.

Walls. The earliest type of all, the wooden wall, continued to be used, especially for dwellings, to the end of the Ottoman period. Generally a framework is first erected of wooden uprights, crossbeams and struts; this is then filled in with dried or baked brick, pointed or plastered over, and faced with wood. As may be seen in the country houses of Ankara, these brick-filled wooden frames produced an effect of rustic work. Another system, by which the two wall-faces are built of lath and plaster with an air-space in the middle, is especially common in the houses of Bursa and Istanbul. The dried and baked brick wall-technique of Mesopotamia and Central Asia continued to be used by the Seljuks, especially in Persia. In order to protect these bricks from the effects of the weather, the sides forming the face of the wall were covered with coloured enamel; in addition geometric patterns and designs helped to produce an artistic ornamentation. This building tradition, seen in the Seljuk türbes and sepulchral towers, survives in Anatolia in minarets, in the drums of domes, and in the walls of eyvans. The technique in question is found in the monuments of Konya and continues in the earliest Ottoman buildings, for example in the minaret of the Green Mosque at İznik and in the Green Türbe at Bursa; it is even seen at Istanbul in the Çinili Köşk. In these buildings it is a mistake to see Persian influence, and to trace their origin wholly to a foreign architecture. They belong in fact to the glazed brick building tradition which the

77, 78

42

110

Seljuks first developed in Persia, then brought to Anatolia and bequeathed to the Ottomans. In the Beylik of Karaman, in the fourteenth century, walls were built of ordinary brick and the outer face coated with marble. The Ottomans on the other hand, in the fifteenth to seventeenth centuries, covered only the inner faces with square tiles 65 (faience); the outer faces were of square blocks. We know further that the Turks possessed the combined stone and brick technique: in the ruins of the Uygur city of Hoço, of the late seventh century, rubble stone walls with mortar are to be seen. The Anatolian Seljuks at Konya maintained this rubble stone building tradition simultaneously with glazed brick decoration, and they faced their walls with squared slabs of stone or marble. This was a distinct advance. These stone walls were slenderer and more resistant, and not only produced a nobler and more truly architectural effect, but were more permanent. Corresponding to local geological conditions, a new stone-working industry sprang up. The early Turkish buildings in India, of similar date, were also of stone. The first Ottoman architects at Bursa used to set small oblong 84 bricks, 3·5 to 4 cm. thick, in the mortar between the joints of their stone walls; they also used raised pointing and a variety of decorative 103 designs in incised lines. The reason for this is to be sought not so much in the influence of Byzantine practice as in the geological poverty of the land and the rough wall technique necessitated by the quality of the available stone. In the time of Beyazıt I and Mehmet I, when the Ottoman territory was richer and more extensive, we find the buildings at Bursa faced with marble and stone slabs. Similarly in the monuments 45, 46 of Edirne and Istanbul the walls are of squared stone blocks. The blocks are secured to one another with metal clamps. Stone walls relieved with courses of brick are found occasionally, but only in secular 88 buildings or modest structures recalling the practice of early Ottoman 107 times.

Pillars and Columns. The Seljuks in Persia made little use of pillars in their massive brick buildings. In Anatolia, on the other hand, the Seljuk halls are usually built on pillars or piers of squared blocks of rectangular or octagonal form. Columns are also used, but rarely. Columns were no doubt originally of wood; indeed, in the Beylik period (fourteenth century) this tradition still survived; we have already noticed it in the mosques of Kastamonu, Beyşehir and Afyon. More 39

frequently than full columns, we find in Seljuk buildings miniature
75 stone columns set in the angles at the sides of the doors. Their shafts are
76 worked into spirals or zigzags and recall the forms of European Romanesque; the capitals are formed of small spheres and leaf or plant designs.
36a Sometimes the Seljuks took pleasure in re-using the columns and
capitals that they found among the ruins of classical antiquity, a custom
familiar among other medieval nations. The original Seljuk capitals are
adorned with 'stalactites' or natural fronds; both forms may be seen in
the Blue Medrese at Sivas. These fronds are not acanthus fronds, nor
are they in high relief or openwork; they are realistically designed and
66 almost flat. Of these capitals the Ottomans adopted and developed only
70 the 'stalactite' type. At the same time they also used a plainer type in
the form of an inverted truncated pyramid with lozenge designs in
low relief; this is derived from the so-called 'Turkish triangle' by means
of which transition was effected to the circle of the dome. This form of
capital is unknown to any Moslem nation but the Turks. The column-
shafts are unfluted and usually monolithic, with bases consisting of a
series of mouldings. The type of capital here described was used in
almost every part of Turkey from the fifteenth to the eighteenth century;
excellent specimens may be seen in the monumental buildings of
68 Edirne and Istanbul. Ottoman pillars and piers are sometimes round and
sometimes have four, six, eight or more sides; they are either of stone
blocks or faced with tiles. The more massive ones are relieved with
niches, pilasters or profiles, and fluting.

101 *Arches*. In both Seljuk and Ottoman architecture the preference is for
108 the broken pointed arch, like a Tudor arch, or the two-centred drop
arch; round arches are rare. This pointed arch was used regularly
from the eleventh century onwards; at an earlier date, in the ninth
century, it may be seen at Samarra and the Uygur city of Hoço. Later
it was adopted in Gothic architecture. Its origin goes back to the
Sumerians. The blocks forming the arches are plain and flat-faced; the
only decoration consists of the alternation of light and dark-coloured
stone and the various shapes given to the joints between them. These
arches are used for arcades and all important openings. Another type
first used at Bursa in the Green and Beyazıt I Mosques, is the shouldered
arch, flat in the middle with a quarter-circle at each side. In some
arcades of the Ottoman period at Bursa and Istanbul ogee arches are to

80

be seen. Segmental arches are used over doors and gateways. The 56
arrangement of two small arches side by side with a column between
them, the whole surmounted by a larger arch (as in fifteenth-century
Venetian buildings), is found in the Karaman period in the Ak Medrese
at Niğde, and in the early Ottoman period in the mosques of Orhan and
Murad I at Bursa. 43

Windows. Both in wooden and stone structures windows are normally
rectangular. In stone buildings relieving arches are placed over the
windows, and the tympanum filled with decoration. In the Seljuk and
Beylik periods the frame has generally 'stalactite' ornamentation. The 46
same is also true of the Ottoman period, except that in the classical age
a plainer style is preferred; the window is merely framed with a moulded
border. Windows are usually arranged in a double horizontal row. 56
The lower row has flat lintels with gratings of bronze or iron, the upper
is arched and filled with stained glass panes, the outside being divided
into plaster partitions of circular or oval shape. This double row of
windows on a single floor gives the façade of Turkish buildings a special 112-120
character of its own.

Doors. In the architecture of every country importance is attached to the
main entrance. In Turkish architecture, however, doors and gates have
an additional value and significance: under the Ottomans, for example,
the Prime Ministerial Department was known as Bab-ı-Âli (High Gate,
Sublime Porte). Accordingly, the gateways in the façades of buildings
are monumental structures, striking to the eye; the door itself is in the
middle at the back of a niche, and is of modest size with lintel and arch.
Gateways are, as it were, smaller versions of the eyvans. In Anatolian
Seljuk gates, as in old woven fabrics, the entire surface is worked;
these façades are the most precious treasure houses of the Seljuk art 81
of sculptured decoration. Among the Ottomans, however, they are to a
lesser degree purely decorative and become comparatively plain and
functional. Nevertheless, with their square or oblong proportions,
central niche with 'stalactite' decoration and corner colonnettes, they 56
continue the Seljuk tradition. The leaves of the doors, like those of the
windows, are generally of wood and carry small decorative panels;
in Seljuk buildings these are normally engraved with plant motifs,
among the Ottomans they are inlaid with geometrical patterns. Those

inlaid with mother-of-pearl are especially fine. Khans, on the other hand, have very large double doors, in which a wicket is inserted. The doors are of iron; that is, iron plates are laid over the wood and secured with huge-headed nails. The bronze work on the outer gate of the Sultan Ahmet Mosque is unusual as well as handsome. Metal fittings, such as lock, key, knocker and handle, display highly skilled craftsmanship.

Roofs. Among the Seljuks the terrace roof was normal, and it is still used in Anatolian houses. The space was first spanned by wooden beams, generally round, laid at short intervals on the stone arches or wooden rafters that joined the pillars. These intervals were then covered over with planks and brushwood, and above this a gently sloping water-proof layer of beaten earth. The roof water was carried off by channels—circular inside, triangular or pentagonal outside—either plain or ending in stylized animals' heads (gargoyles). Among the Ottomans wooden roofs gently sloping on four sides, covered with lead or Turkish-style roof-tiles, were in common use. An essential feature of this architectural style is the wide eaves projecting several metres beyond the outer wall of the building. These recall Chinese roofs, but instead of turning up at the edges they are either straight or even hang downwards; the under-surface is of wood and is decorated in colour. The Seljuks also experimented with domed roofs but this style was only fully developed by the Ottomans. The dome is hemispherical in form, constructed of brick, plastered on the inside, and covered on the outside with lead, or in early times with tiles. In mosques the circular dome rests on a rectangular arcade open or closed, in other buildings (as for example in the Eski Kaplıca at Bursa and the türbe of Selim II in Istanbul) on an octagonal arcade within a rectangle, the transition being effected by pendentives. In the case of rectangular areas enclosed by massive walls, the dome rests either on an octagonal base formed by *trompes* or on a polygonal cornice formed by 'stalactites' and 'Turkish triangles' (so called because they are not found outside Turkish architecture). This building style goes back to an Uygur prototype 500 years earlier. The vaulted and domed construction found in the stupa and other ruins at Hoço is derived from construction in wood, as may be seen in the cave ceilings of Kızıl. The Sassanid technique afforded the latest model for Seljuk constructional art. In the Seljuk tombs in Persia we find sharp-pointed

82

bulbiform domes divided into sections; but these had no great vogue in Anatolia. On the other hand, the style which comprises, internally and externally, a dome set on a drum, as in the türbe of Sultan Sencer at Merv (1157), became a lasting tradition. The Anatolian Seljuk mausolea 20 were roofed internally with a light flattish dome, and externally with a 29 conical stone roof. The Ottomans continued this tradition in the form of an externally loftier dome, as in the türbes of Süleyman the Magnificent, Kılıç Ali Pasha and Selim II. These have a double dome higher 64 outside than in, but in general among the Ottomans a single dome, of such proportions as to produce internally and externally a satisfying effect, became the norm. The summit of the dome is usually crowned by an emblem (acroterion) overlaid with real gold; this may take the form of a small dome, a star and crescent, a tulip or a series of mouldings. In some cases the top of the dome has a lantern orifice for the admission of light and air; these are polygonal in shape and covered over with a small dome or conical roof. The lateral thrust of large domes was met by the addition of towers, ordinary or flying buttresses, or half-domes. In secular buildings such as schools and markets, and sometimes in türbes, pointed cradle vaults or cross-vaults were employed, either plain or ribbed; over these was placed a sloping roof, and the intermediate space filled with rubble.

Ornamentation. Turkish architecture has multi-coloured decoration with a rich variety of motifs; it is worked either in the form of a flat surface or in relief. In order to understand the motifs and the style of composition, it is necessary briefly to recall their origins in pre-islamic Turkish art. From the Bronze Age onwards decoration comprising animal figures, scrolls and fronds held an important place in the cultural media of the Central Asiatic Turks. Together with them occur abstract geometrical figures. From the stylization of the animal figures in plant form arose the zoomorphic style. In the door of the Gazneli Mahmut türbe it is interesting to see the stucco technique and style of the houses at Samarra (a Turkish garrison town) and, within a six-pointed star, the same decorative style as in the walls and ceilings of Bezeklik in the Tarım Basin. Further, the Kufic script on the towers of Gazneli Mahmut and Mes'ud must rank as decoration. We shall attempt to indicate how this art was brought to Anatolia by the Seljuks, close kindred of the Gaznelis, and thence passed on to the Ottoman Empire.

In the türbe of Keykâvus inside the Seljuk hospital at Sivas, the decorative motifs of the glazed tilework comprise, alongside geometrical patterns, the gammadion (or swastika), eight-pointed stars, Arabesque and Kufic inscriptions. The gammadion is known thousands of years earlier in Sumeria and as a relic of the Hittites in Anatolia. On the tombs and among the symbols of the Turkish tribes of Central Asia we find also the cross. Long before it became a Christian emblem the cross existed as an ornamental motif. The gammadion continues to be used, in various distorted forms, in the castle at Diyarbakır, in the gateway of the Karatay Medrese at Konya, and on the doors of nearly all Seljuk and Ottoman buildings. The carved animal and human figures in the Blue Medrese and Şifaiye at Sivas, in the mosque of Divriği, the mausolea of Kayseri and Niğde, the castle of Diyarbakır and many other

89, 91 Seljuk monuments, are a continuation of the old Turkish animal style. The Ottomans also maintained this tradition, adding zoomorphic forms to the plant decoration of the Seljuks. This is known as the Rumî or Seljukid style; it occurs in a great variety of designs either as relief on

93 marble or stucco or painted on ceilings and faience tiles. In this style the tendrils take scroll form and the leaves turn to animals' paws or horns, or birds' beaks. The Hataî style comprises naturalistic compositions of scrolls drawn with fine lines, together with rosettes, flowers and leaves. This style is seen in the Timurid buildings of Samarkand, Horasan and other cities, and at the same date (fifteenth century) in the Green Mosque at Bursa, reckoned as one of the earliest Ottoman buildings. In the sixteenth and seventeenth centuries it was used for Persian carpets. As its name implies, it derives its origin from the art of eastern Turkistan and China. Geometrical shapes also, notably the triangle and hexagon, are used in honeycomb form in terracotta pave-

48 ments and in faience wall facings. As variants of these a number of star forms were evolved and used for relief or engraving on wood or for open iron and stonework, producing highly artistic panels, railings and balustrades. Although these designs are common to almost all eastern architecture, they are for some reason or other called 'arabesque' by

65 Western nations. Among these plant and flower designs, particularly in Ottoman works of the sixteenth and seventeenth centuries, we find especially, half-realistic and half-stylized cypress trees, geraniums, bean and ivy leaves, rose, hyacinth, carnation and tulip. Together with the 'pomegranate pip' (which also occurs in Chinese art), dishes of

84

pears, peaches and other fruits are shown in Ottoman works in the form
of reliefs devoid of perspective; these are especially common on fountains
of the Tulip Period. In the Empire and Baroque Periods, when Euro-
peanism was the fashion, these purely Turkish motifs which we have
briefly described gave way to French motifs; so strong, however, was
the old tradition that these acquired a Turkish character. Towards the
end of the Ottoman period the old Turkish decoration reappeared in
combination with neo-classical architectural forms. Of the various
styles of writing, the square Kufic script, being particularly well adapted
for mosaic, was found most appropriate for Seljuk faience. It continued 74
to be used by the Ottomans also, in the form of mosaic writing on
stone, but for inscriptions and friezes the Sülüs and Celî scripts are 65
much commoner. These scripts were not mixed with other ornamentation, as they were by the Arabs, but remained a pure and independent
art.

Seljuk Faience, which includes all these motifs, was applied in two
ways, either in the form of pieces cut from a larger tile slab, or in
mosaic form; the colours used were turquoise, lapis-lazuli, black and
brown. That lustrous tiles, first made under Turkish rule at Samarra,
spread from Egypt to Spain, Rak'â and Persia, was already well known;
now they have appeared also at Konya, in the excavations at the hill
of Alâüddin and Kubâd-âbâd. In these the prevailing colours are white
and green; they are applied to the walls in the form of oblongs, crosses
and eight-pointed stars. A noteworthy feature is the occurrence of male
and female figures in squatting posture, as in the Uygur paintings.
Similar designs are to be seen on the Rey faience in the Istanbul museum
and the Kâşan plates illustrated in Pope's book. From the name of this
latter city comes the term kâşî, formerly applied by the Seljuks to
faience. The occurrence of these designs in Anatolia therefore provides
the final link in the chain of western Asiatic Seljuk art. The Ottomans
also continued to use this Seljuk technique, as in the tiles of the Green
Mosques at İznik and Bursa and finally in the Çinili Köşk at Istanbul.
Throughout the sixteenth and seventeenth centuries, tiles from the
furnaces of İznik and Kütahya were applied to the walls of mosques and 65
palaces. The predominant colours are dark blue, turquoise, green and 113
scarlet. Early in the eighteenth century this art begins to decline, and
its place is taken by Viennese and Italian faience.

The Ottoman architects preferred simplicity in their ornamentation,

85

and aimed at a balance between blank and decorated surfaces. Seljuk art, on the other hand, ran somewhat to extravagance and avoided flat empty spaces.

Workmen and Workmanship. During the period of the Turkish migrations many artists and craftsmen settled and remained in the neighbouring countries of the east. While Persia, Iraq, Egypt and Syria were under Turkish rule, the part played by Turkish workmen in carrying their own art and architectural forms to these countries is easily understood. They it was that transformed a downfallen, second-rate town like Konya (Iconium) into a Turkish Moslem capital city, and founded so many new cities on the Central Asiatic model. This was the work of emigrants from the cities of Turkistan who settled here in early times and were later reinforced by the Turkish artisans who followed the invading armies on their march from east to west. On some Seljuk buildings may be seen the names of craftsmen from Damascus, Aleppo and Ahlat. This is a result of the exchange system practised by the Moslem Artists' Corporation, just as in Europe at the same period such exchanges were common. In the same way, the similarity of plan and tiled decoration observable between the buildings of Samarkand, Horasan and Kâşan on the one hand, and the contemporary monuments of Bursa on the other, is explained by these contacts and exchanges of artists and craftsmen. As a typical example, the great Sinan in the sixteenth century, on request, sent his own architects to construct the monuments of Agra. At the same time there was nothing to prevent the employment of local Christian artisans; this, however, only became common in the eighteenth and nineteenth centuries, when the true Turkish architectural character had entered a cosmopolitan phase.

Among the archives of the Topkapı Palace have been found the plans and estimates of the Ottoman architects; a list of designers working under the architects has also come to light. We have for example the Sultan's firman, issued to the city of İznik, ordering the manufacture and dispatch to Istanbul of tiles conforming to these designers' sketches. These documents give us an idea of the working conditions of the time.

CHAPTER FOUR

AESTHETIC CONSIDERATIONS

Both in religious and civil architecture, the height of the building is much less than its length. This horizontal effect gives an impression of comfort and repose, to which the perpendicular minaret in a mosque 61 affords a pleasing contrast. In religious buildings the solid parts pre- 69 dominate over the window-openings; this derives from a massive building style. In secular architecture on the other hand, in houses and 119 pavilions, the window-strips dominate the entire façade; this produces 120 a cheerful effect, in achieving which the old framework technique of wooden buildings was of considerable assistance. Seljuk and Ottoman 114 architects alike avoided perfect symmetry in their ground plans and façades; even in buildings which look symmetrical many irregularities 102, 104 are in fact present. Rather than bind themselves slavishly to rules, they preferred the dictates of practical necessity and utility. Their architecture, even in the matter of ornamentation, is wholly rational and constructional. The acroteria at the summit of domes and minarets serve the purpose of covering the joints of the lead sheets over the roof; 'stalactites' are minature prismatic consoles used to effect transition to a projecting surface; the geometrically designed brick courses in wall-faces have the 43 function of reinforcing the rubble masonry; the glazed and coloured tiles with which walls were faced afforded better protection against the weather. In this fundamental field Ottoman architecture strove above all to produce an effect of beauty by means of harmony of proportion. Its architectural elements display a variety of proportion, but in general the essential parts are on a scale adapted to human needs. For example, 56 gateways are built high for monumental effect, but the actual door is of normal size.

The columns at the side of the Şehzade Mosque are spaced at intervals equal to half their height; in the dome of the Süleymaniye Mosque also

87

the proportion is 1:2. In arches the proportion of width to height is generally 3:5 or 5:8; in windows it is 5:8, 4:7 or 6:11. In the side-arcades of the Selimiye and Süleymaniye Mosques monotony is avoided by alternation of broad and narrow arches. In the Süleymaniye Mosque the intervals between the three balconies (*şerefe*) of the minarets increase upwards in proportion; at the same time the thickness of the shaft of the minaret decreases in each of these intervals by 10 cm. The two minarets of the Mihrimah Mosque at Üsküdar are unequal in diameter. These random examples give an idea of the standards of proportion and perspective which were applied.

Externally, all that meets the eye is simple forms, mouldings and reliefs, suited to their place and adapted to the nature of the material. The interiors on the other hand, with their stained glass, tiles, carpets, stucco ornaments and inscriptions, are much richer and more colourful. In türbes and mosques the internal and external spaces are as pure and harmonious as a soap-bubble; and their fine-cut, crystal-sharp outlines appear as if designed within the frame of a triangle. The groups of mosques and other independent buildings were set among trees and greenery in such a way as not to destroy the natural amenities. As residential areas developed around them they became veritable city centres. All this underlines the important part town planning played in Turkish architecture.

88

CHAPTER FIVE

COMPARISON AND CONCLUSION

In order to reach a sound conclusion it would be desirable to make a comparative study of Turkish art before and after the acceptance of Islam. Until the beginning of the twentieth century no research was made into the history of Turkish art. The political conditions since, resulting from two world wars, have unfortunately hindered the progress of these studies. Concerning the ultimate origins of Turkish architectural art various hypotheses of dubious validity have been put forward; nor is the case much better with regard to the Islamic period. Very soon after the adoption of Islamism the Turks found themselves engaged in the government and defence of the whole Moslem world from India to Spain. Intermingling with all these nations, they brought to them their own structural forms, their own artists and workmen. How much did they contribute to the architecture of these nations, and how much did they take from them? This essential question has unfortunately hardly been examined scientifically. For ourselves, we cannot accept that Turkish architecture is derived from that of India, Persia, Georgia and Arabia. This would be to fall into the error of those who see in it nothing that cannot be attributed to the art of Syria, Persia and Byzantium. Certain historians of western and Hellenistic art, having begun their studies with Arabian and Persian art, have fallen victims to preconceived notions of its priority. Can it be right, in defiance of all the human, social and physical conditions which affect the form of architecture, to lump together under the name of Islamic art the architecture of all Moslem nations, simply by reason of their common religion? Shall we class together the Romanesque, Gothic and Renaissance architecture of the various European nations under the heading of Christian art? On the contrary, we distinguish French and English Gothic, English and Italian Renaissance. All employ the same arches,

89

domes, vaults and columns; but to the discerning eye each has its individual character. Indeed, even within the architecture of a single nation there are distinctive differences of period, as for example the Quatrocento and Cinquecento periods in Italian Renaissance. In the same way Islamic architectures, Arabian, Persian, Turkish—even Seljuk and Ottoman Turkish—are each an independent art with characteristic features that distinguish it from the others. Let the reader look at pictures of the Kâidbey Mosque at Cairo, the Mescidi Şah Mosque at Ispahan, and the Şehzade Mosque at Istanbul. If we consider only the external features, minaret and domes, the differences of character are unmistakable. They may be summarized thus:

TURKISH	ARABIAN	PERSIAN
1. Perspicuous form and monumental effect.	1. Confused and complicated form.	1. Decorative form and effect.
2. Modest harmonious proportions.	2. Irregular proportions.	2. Disproportion.
3. Simple and clear conception.	3. Intricate geometrical conception.	3. Fantastic and poetical conception.
4. Character appropriate to the nature of the material.	4. Character irrespective of the nature of the material.	4. Character adapted to the material.
5. Effects of space, with light and shade.	5. Geometrical surface decoration.	5. Surface decoration in colour.
6. Moderation in ornament.	6. Extravagant ornamentation.	6. Crowded ornamentation.

A similar comparison (which has now become almost commonplace) between a monument of Justinian and one of Turkish Istanbul, will yield the same result. The mosque of Sultan Ahmet might indeed have been built against St. Sophia expressly for purposes of comparison.

SULTAN AHMET	ST. SOPHIA
1. Plastic and stereometric form.	1. Solid unadorned mass.
2. Conspicuous hemispherical dome.	2. Low and inconspicuous circular dome.
3. Exterior takes its form from the interior.	3. Total disregard of exterior appearance.
4. Constructional elements disguised by the architectural forms.	4. Exterior rendered ponderous by buttress walls.
5. Tiles of contrasting colours.	5. Gilt mosaics.

90

SULTAN AHMET (*continued*)	ST. SOPHIA (*continued*)
6. Geometric column-capitals and arcades with pointed arches.	6. Round arches supported on columns with openwork capitals.
7. Perfect centralization in plan and spacing.	7. Central dome eccentric to general plan.
8. Surface unity; uniformity of plan uninterrupted by subdivisions.	8. Basilical form, with side-naves cut off from the central nave.

The arrangement comprising one dome and two half-domes, which is common to the mosques of Istanbul and to St. Sophia is, as we saw above in the section devoted to mosques, a natural result of the historical evolution of Turkish architecture.

Byzantine architecture is closely allied to the Graeco-Roman tradition and much influenced by the Early Christian architecture of western Asia and Asia Minor. Ottoman Turkish architecture, on the other hand, is allied to the Far Eastern and Central Asiatic tradition, and is under the influence not only of Western Asia and Anatolia, but also of Mesopotamian and Sassanid art. The two are distinct in respect of culture and origin, and unite, in accordance with geographical conditions, under the influence of the old architecture of the East.

Not a single Seljuk mosque was converted from a church or raised on the ruins of a church; they are without exception built on new foundations of their own. Not only mosques, but medreses, türbes, khans, houses and palaces, conformed to their own traditional forms and formulas, adapted to the requirements of climate and the available materials. The history of architecture all over the world is replete with examples of the influence exerted by one art upon another; but this is not to deny that every art has its own original individuality. So regarded, Turkish architecture will be found to be as original as any other.

This conclusion might have been strengthened if we could have entered into questions of scientific and technical method; but these lie beyond the scope of the present modest essay. We have been obliged to confine ourselves to a somewhat artificial tabular form of presentation. If within these limits we have succeeded in clarifying the matters at issue, we shall be well content. For any shortcomings we ask indulgence.

SOME WELL-KNOWN TURKISH ARCHITECTS

Bizl Oğlu Mehmet, of Merend. His name is written on the türbe of Keykâvus in the medical school at Sivas (1220). Decorative architect.

Osman Oğlu Mehmet, of Tus. Built the Sırçalı Medrese at Konya (1242).

Abdullah Oğlu Kelük. Among his works are the Sahib Atâ Mosque at Konya (1258), the İnce Minare Theological School (1279), and the Gök Medrese at Sivas (1272).

Hüseyin Oğlu Ali. His name is on the türbe of Yıldırım Beyazıt at Bursa (1406).

Hacı Ivaz. Built the Green Mosque at Bursa (1419), a masterpiece of Turkish architecture. From his tombstone we learn that he was also a field-commander, scholar and mathematician. Son of Ahî-Beyazıt. Died 1427.

Hacı Alâüddin, of Konya. Between the years 1400 and 1422 built many mosques, bridges, khans and baths at Bursa and Edirne. He was among the artists responsible for the revolution in Ottoman architecture.

Atîk Sinan. Royal architect of the period of Mehmet the Conqueror. Founded the original Fâtih Mosque and its surrounding buildings. He was buried in the courtyard of the Kumrulu Mescit, which he himself built (1471). İlyas Ağa (died 1486) was a distinguished member of his team of architects.

Hayrüddin. Architect of the mosque of Beyazıt II, the earliest monumental work in Istanbul (1501). But the Royal Architect of Beyazıt II was Yakub Şah.

Esir Ali. A Turk of Azerbaijan, brought to Istanbul by Sultan Selim I on his return from his Persian triumph, and for this reason also called Acem Ali. The mosque of Sultan Selim at Istanbul and that of Safyüddin in Bulgaria are among his characteristic works. He was buried at Istanbul in the Mimar Camii which he built himself in the region of Şehremini (1537).

Koca Sinan, master architect. Born in 1490 in Central Anatolia at the village of Ağırnas in the vilâyet of Kayseri. His grandfather Doğan Yusuf Ağa was a builder, and in the course of business took Sinan to visit the Seljuk monuments in Kayseri and the neighbourhood. At the age of 22 Sinan was brought to Istanbul and was instructed at the Palace in the Hippodrome. A year later he was accepted into the Enderun (Primary Military School) in the same quarter. In the years 1514–1516, in the course of his travels with the army of Selim I, he had the opportunity to inspect the Turkish and Persian domed buildings of Tebriz, and to wander among the works of arabesque art in Cairo. He finished his training in 1520, and became Constructional Officer in the Janissaries. In the 23 years of his army career he achieved great success in such military technical works as castles, fortifications and bridges. With the knowledge and experience thus gained we find him at the age of 47 in full activity as chief of the corps of architects of a great empire. For 52 years he worked with his colleagues in the construction of buildings, and erected in various parts of the empire some 360 monuments. By his desire he was buried in the garden of his house close to his own Süleymaniye Mosque that he loved so well (1588). He has been compared with Michael Angelo (1475–1564), his contemporary both in age and in period of activity; but a better comparison, despite the interval of time between them, would probably be with the English architect Christopher Wren (1632–1723). Both were country lads; both possessed exceptional ability, and were past their first youth when they turned to architecture; both were highly prolific and long-lived, and remained active to the end of their days. In their early days Sinan occupied himself with military engineering, Wren with mathematics and astronomy. One left his mark on Protestant English, the other on Turkish Islamic architecture.

Davut Ağa. Succeeded Sinan as royal architect (1587), died 1599. His masterpiece is the Yeni Cami at Eminönü (Istanbul).

Dalgıç Ahmet. Chief architect from 1599 to 1604; died 1607. His finest work is the mausoleum of Murad II beside St. Sophia.

Kasım Ağa. Became chief architect in 1622. His Çinili Cami at Üsküdar is much admired, but his masterpiece is considered to be the Baghdad Pavilion and terrace in the Topkapı Palace (1638).

Mehmet Ağa. His masterpiece is the Sultan Ahmet Mosque at Istanbul. He came to Istanbul in 1567, and studied music, then architecture. He succeeded Dalgıç Ahmet as royal architect in 1606. In a book on architectural theory entitled *Handbook of Architecture* (*Risalei-Mimariye*), written for him by Cafer Efendi, he gives a comprehensive account of the methods of work and architectural training in vogue at that period.

Elhac Mehmet Ağa. Architect of the Sultan Ahmet Fountain (1728) and many other fountains. On his death in 1742 he was buried at the Adrianople Gate.

Çelebi Mustafa. Chief architect in 1755. Employed the Baroque style in the Nuru Osmaniye Mosque, Medrese and Hospice in Istanbul. He was assisted by his apprentice Simon Kalfa.

Mehmet Tahir Ağa. Royal architect 1764–1767. It was he who adapted the Baroque and Rococo styles to Turkish architecture. He was responsible for the present Fâtih Mosque, the work being superintended by his apprentice Kör Yani.

Professor Kemaleddin. Studied architecture at Charlottenburg and taught at Istanbul in the Engineering School and Academy of Fine Arts. He built many mosques, türbes and khans. Died in 1927 at the age of 57.

Mehmet Vedat Bey. Studied in Paris and became chief architect to Sultan Reşad in 1920. Taught in the Academy of Fine Arts at Istanbul. Together with Kemaleddin Bey he worked for the renaissance of Turkish architecture. Among many of his works in Istanbul the new post office is the most successful. Died 1942. His pupil Muzaffer is the architect of the Monument of Liberty.

SHORT BIBLIOGRAPHY

This bibliography is not exhaustive. It comprises a selection of the most recent works in various languages of which use has been made in the present study.

GENERAL

ARSEVEN. C. E., *L'art Turc*, Istanbul 1939.

—*Les Arts Décoratives Turc*, Istanbul 1952.

CRESSWELL. K. A. C., *Early Muslim Architecture II*, Oxford 1940.

EGLI. E., *Sinan*, Zürich 1954.

GODARD. A., *Khorasan*, ATHAR-E-IRAN IV, 1949.

MILLINGEN. A. VAN, *Constantinople*, London 1906.

RICE. T., *Some Near Eastern Elements in Western Architecture*, THE ARCHITECTURAL REVIEW V, 78.

SANDERSON. J., *The Travels of J. Sanderson in the Levant*, London 1931.

SCHLUMBERGER. D., *The Ghaznevid Palace*, ILLUSTRATED LONDON NEWS, March 25th, 1950, June 16th, 1951.

STRZYGOWSKI. J., *Altai, Iran*, Leipzig 1917.

—*Türkler ve Orta Asya Sanatı Meselesi*, TÜRKIYAT MEC. C. II, Istanbul 1930.

ÜNSAL. B., *Mimarî Tarihi*, Istanbul 1949.

SELJUK PERIOD

AĞAOĞLU. M., *Unpublished Wooden Doors of the Seljuq Period*, PARNASSUS X, 1938.

ARSEVEN. C. E., *Türk Sanatı Tarihi* II–III, Istanbul 1954.

ETHEM. H., *Anadolu'da Selçuklu Abideleri*, Ankara 1947.

GABRIEL. A., *Monuments Turc d'Anatolie I–II*, Paris 1931–1934.

—*Voyages Archéologiques dans la Turquie Orientale*, Paris 1940.

SARRE. F., *Konia, Seldchukische Baudenkmäler*, Berlin 1921.

SCHROEDER. E., *The Seljuq Period* (*A Survey of Persian Art*, A. U. Pope) V.II, Oxford 1939.

BEYLİK PERIOD

ALSANAPA-DIEZ. E., KOMAN. M., *Karaman Devri Sanatı*, Istanbul 1950.

RIEFSTAHL. R. M., *Turkish Architecture in South-western Anatolia*, Cambridge 1931.

ÜLGEN. A. S., *Niğde'de Ak Medrese*, VAKIFLAR DERGİSİ II, Ankara 1942.

OTTOMAN PERIOD

AĞAOĞLU. M., *The Fâtih Mosque at Constantinople*, ART BULLETIN XII, 1930.

ANHEGGER. R., *Beiträge zur Frühosmanischen Baugeschichte*, Istanbul 1953.

ALSANAPA. O., *Edirne'de Osmanlı Devri Abideleri*, Istanbul 1954.

—*Macaristan'da Türk Abideleri*, TARİH DERGİSİ I, Istanbul 1950.

AYVERDİ. E. H., *Fâtih Devri Mimârîsi*, Istanbul 1953.

—*Yugoslavya'da Türk Abideleri*, VAKIFLAR DERGİSİ III, Ankara 1956.

BALDUCCI. H., *Architettura Turca in Rodi*, Milano 1932.

ÇETİNTAS. S., *Türk Mimarî Anitları, Bursa'da Ilk Eserler*, Istanbul 1946.

ETHEM. H., *Topkapı Sarayı*, Istanbul 1931.

EYİCE. S., *Yunanistan'da Türk Mimarî Eserleri*, TÜRKİYAT MEC. XI–XII, 1954–1955.

GABRIEL. A., *Les Mosquées de Constantinople*, SYRIA VII, 1926.

—*Châteaux Turc du Bosphore*, Paris 1943.

GLÜCK. H., *Die Bäder Constantinopels*, Wien 1921.

GÖKNİL-VOGT. U., *Les Mosquées Turques*, Zürich 1953.

KLINGHARDT, K., *Türkische Bäder*, Stuttgart 1927.

MINETTI. H., *Osmanische Provinziale Baukunst auf dem Balkan*, Hanover 1923.

SÖYLEMEZOĞLU. K., *Islam Dini, Ilk Camiler ve Osmanlı Camileri*, Istanbul 1955.

ÜLGEN. A. S., *Kirşehir'de Türk Eserleri, Yeni Cami, Ahmet Paşa Heyeti*, VAKIFLAR DERGİSİ II, Ankara 1942.

—*Iznik'te Türk Eserleri*, VAKIFLAR DERGİSİ I, Ankara 1938.

ÜNSAL. B., *Iznik Ciniciligine dair*, MESLEKİ TEKNIK OGRETIM DERGİSİ 37–38, 1956.

SHORT GLOSSARY

Arasta. Open or covered market.

Bedesten. Domed covered market, supported internally as a rule by pillars.

Bimârhane. Mental hospital.

Cami. A larger mosque.

Caravanserai. A road guest house, an equivalent to the modern motel.

Çarşı. A market hall, grand bazaar.

Çeşme. A public fountain.

Cumba. Floor projecting beyond the floor below.

Eyvan. A vaulted recess with three sides enclosed.

Hamam. Public bath.

Han (khan, inn). Lodging house for travellers, merchants and postal convoys.

Harem. Women's quarters.

Hisar. Fortified castle, tower.

Imaret. Hospice.

Kaplıca. Thermal baths.

Kasr. Country house, château.

Khan. *See* han.

Konak. A larger and richer type of house.

Köşk. A pavilion set in a summer garden.

Kümbet. A turret-tomb with a high drum and conical dome.

Medrese. Theological school and educational building.

Mescit. A small mosque.

Mihrab. A niche in the wall of the prayer hall which points towards Mecca and is thus always in front of the congregation at prayer.

Minare. Signal post, used by the priests to call the faithful to prayer.

Minber. A pulpit.

Şadırvan. A kind of fountain for ritual ablution in the court of a mosque or medrese.

Saray. Palace, Serai.

Sebil. A free water and fruit-juice drinking institution.

Selamlık. Men's quarters.

Şifahane (or Şifaiye). A hospital.

Sırça. Glazed bricks.

Tabhane. Convalescent home for Moslem priests.

Tekke. A convent.

Türbe. A mausoleum.

Yalı. A seashore residence.

DESCRIPTIVE NOTES TO PHOTOGRAPHS

35. Alâüddin Mosque at Konya. Built on a hill and skilfully adapted to the slope of the ground. The group of mosque, türbe, cistern, and court surrounded by walls and platform, is suggestive of a medieval castle. The work was completed by Alâüddin Keykûbad I. The decagonal türbe with its pyramid roof is reminiscent of the mausolea of western Asia, and by its architectural form dominates the whole composition.

36. The interior arcades of this mosque are supported on 62 columns, which (as often in medieval architecture) have been taken from the ruins of ancient buildings. The central part of the mosque dates to the time of Mesud I. The pulpit, of the time of Kılıçarslan II, is most artistically worked in ebony with geometric designs. Some of the titles of the mihrab and the base of the dome have fallen away. The mosque underwent modification at the time of its repair in 1889.

37. Ulu Cami at Divriği. Entered by two gateways; the decoration of that on the north has a tendency towards Indian style. Its appliqué motifs are inorganic and ill-suited to the material; they are suggestive of knitted or woven designs. In the middle of the mosque is an octagonal water-basin and above this a dome open to the sky. The mosque has been much repaired.

38. Interior of the mental hospital at Divriği. Designed and built in conjunction with the mosque. The inscription records that it was built by Turan Melik, daughter of Shah Said Behram. It is a hospital of typical eyvan type. In the interior, the pointed arches and the geometric ornamentaion of the pillars is characteristic. On the other hand, the form of the gateway with its pointed arch is exceptional. Craftsmen from Tiflis and Ahlat worked on both buildings.

39. Interior of the mosque of Mahmut Bey, in the village of Kasaba, 17 km. from Kastamonu. Built by Mahmut Bey, of the family of Çandar. This modest work is significant in a number of ways, e.g. the survival of the Anatolian Hittite building style and hilani tradition, and the contrast between the simplicity of the exterior and the rich interior architecture.

40. Ulu Cami at Bursa. Begun by Murad I and finished by Beyazıt I. It differs from the normal Seljuk mosque not only in being roofed with domes, but also in its dimensions: the cornice-moulding is 16 m. from the ground, and the pillars are 8 m. high; the domes are 23 m.

high and 10 m. in diameter. In the main minaret, which is of brick, are separate staircases for entrance and exit. By repeating on the stone façade the rows of arches in the interior, a lively effect of light and shade has been produced. The pulpit is a masterpiece of woodwork; its pillars are adorned with 192 inscriptions.

41. Şadırvan of the Ulu Cami. Here is the largest of the interior fountains and waterbasins in any of the mosques at Bursa. The windows with their coloured decoration, the façade of the mihrab, the religious enthusiasm of the faithful performing their ablutions to the music of the rippling water beneath the open dome and groups of lights, make an attractive picture.

42. Green Mosque at İznik. Built by the architect Hadjı Musa for Kara Halil Pasha of Çandar. The pointed roof of the minaret is lead-covered, the shaft, balconies and 'stalactites' are veneered with brick or incrusted tiles; this style of construction and design carries on the Seljuk tradition. The prevailing green colour of the tiles has given the building its name. The interior is veneered with marble.

43. Mosque of Murad I at Bursa. Critics observe that the façade is not suggestive of a mosque; this is true enough, since the upper storey is a medrese, of which the balcony arcades in the façade form the open hall; while the ground floor is a department of State containing a place of prayer. The building is, in fact, of a wholly secular character, and is put together in masterly fashion. The use of Byzantine capitals taken from the ruins of ancient buildings is quite in accordance with the fashion of the time.

44. Yıldırım Mosque at Bursa. The work was begun by Yıldırım Beyazıt I (1390), interrupted by the invasion of Tamerlane, and completed in the time of Mehmet I (1402–1421). The mosque, medrese, cookhouse, türbe, hospital, guest-room, baths and castle together formed an independent town. The plan is of the Orhan Camii type, and furnished the model for Bursa's masterpiece, the Green Mosque.

45. Side views of the same mosque. The form of the arches that join the pillars of the façade are original. This type of arch, adapted from construction in wood, is called the Bursa arch. The building is of stone blocks. The Seljuk artisans who worked on this structure created, beside the Anatolian tradition, a new Ottoman architecture.

46. Green Mosque at Bursa. Begun by Çelebi Mehmet in 1415 but not finished. Completed by Murad II in 1421; but certain indications on the façade suggest that it is still unfinished. Its plan includes, besides the place of prayer, a medrese with eyvans, rooms with hearths, halls with water-basins, and a half-floor reserved for the Sultan. It is therefore not an independent mosque, but rather a department of State including a medrese and mosque. The window-frames, adorned with reliefs, in the marble-covered façades are deserving of notice.

47. Green Mosque, from the rear. The modern French architect Le Corbusier quotes this building as a

model of spacing, lighting, colour and rhythm, and praises the harmony of the internal and external architecture with the general plan (*Vers une Architecture*, p. 147).

48. Green Mosque, interior. A world of light and colour. The architect was Ivaz Pasha, the tiling is due to Mehmet Mecnun, the painting and plaster-work to İlyas Ali, and the woodwork to Tebrizî Mehmet. The Turkish architects repeated the plan in its essentials 15 years later in the Blue Mescit at Tabriz. This is evidence that Ottoman Turkish art and the art of Karakoyun go back to a common origin.

49. Green Mosque, Sultan's Lodge. Emphasized by the tiling that covers it on all sides, this building carries on the Seljuk tradition and technique. A concealed staircase runs up inside the wall to this upper floor. The shape of the arch, and the prismatic forms employed for the transition to the round dome, are features peculiar to the Bursa period of Ottoman architecture.

50. Old Mosque at Edirne. Roofed with nine co-ordinated domes. The plan is a fore-runner of the Istanbul mosques, except that the latter have wider spaces between the four pillars and a larger central dome. The front is equipped with arcades. Of the two minarets one rises from the ground, the other from the roof. The building is of squared stone blocks; it was begun by Süleyman Çelebi and finished by Mehmet I. The architect was Hacı Alâüddin of Konya.

51. Üç Şerefeli Mosque at Edirne. Built in the time of Sultan Murad II.

The work was superintended by Ahmet Bey, but the name of the architect is unfortunately not known. This monument, evolutional and transitional, brought the Turkish mosque, in respect of plan, technique and dimensions, to the ideal of perfection. Above six arches, supported by two hexagonal pillars and wall pilasters, rises a large central dome; the diameter is 24 m., as compared with 13 m. in the Old Mosque. The dome is strengthened by iron hoops, the drum by battered arches, a technique not found in Anatolia, Persia or elsewhere. The plan is perfectly centralized.

52. Courtyard and exterior of the same mosque. This courtyard motif had already been used in the Beylik period, but here it has become an organic feature of the architecture. The court is enclosed by four minarets, whose spiral shafts with coloured brick designs keep the Seljuk tradition alive. One of them, 67·62 m. plus 12 m. high, has three balconies and three separate staircases; it is the first minaret of this kind in the Moslem and Turkish world. Another has two balconies approached by separate staircases interwoven within the shaft; this type had already been used in the Old Mosque. The arch over the mihrab, by its decoration, tiles and composition, is reminiscent of the gateways of western Asia.

53. Fâtih Mosque at Istanbul. A large part of the original Fâtih Mosque was destroyed by an earthquake in 1765. Sultan Mustafa III in 1771 removed the ruined portion and rebuilt it on an enlarged scale in its

present form. The new Turkish-Baroque style makes an attractive silhouette.

54. Fâtih Mosque, courtyard. A work of the pre-classical period that survived the earthquake, it was preserved unchanged when the Baroque renovation was undertaken. The court, surrounded by arcades supported on columns, and the conical-roofed şadırvan among upright trees, is highly original; it carries on the old Central Asiatic form and the Seljuk tradition of urban architecture.

55. Mosque of Beyazıt II at Istanbul. The projecting wings behind the courtyard give an effect of Bursa School style to the exterior perspective. The position of the minarets at the outer corners of these projections and apart from the main body of the building is remarkable, but is paralleled in the Mosque of Beyazıt II at Edirne.

56. Same mosque, courtyard gate. In comparison with the Seljuk gateways this gate, with its simple form and proportions, is a specimen of pure architecture, devoid of decoration. This and two other gates give access to the courtyard, from which the mosque is entered. The courtyard has the effect of detaching a man's mind from the material world and preparing it for the spiritual atmosphere of the mosque.

57. Şehzade Mosque at Istanbul. Constructed by Süleyman the Magnificent to honour the memory of his son, Prince Mehmet, untimely put to death. The occasional inorganic elements scattered here and there in the façade of this mosque may be attributed to the architect's feeling for the memory of this unhappy youth.

58. Same mosque, from the rear. The domes rising like a pyramid based on the mass of the building give a stereometric effect. In respect of character and expressiveness in the external architecture, what a gulf divides this monument from St. Sophia!

59. Ulu Cami at Elbistan. This monument from the Beylik period was built 50 years before the Şehzade Mosque. It affords a primitive example of a large central dome supported by four half-domes, and is important as evidence that the conception of a centralized plan was earlier than the Şehzade Mosque. It was Sinan who gave this conception monumental form.

60. Süleymaniye Mosque at Istanbul. Sinan was an architect who brought earlier conceptions to the pinnacle of art. So in the present case the plan is taken from the Mosque of Beyazıt II, a work of Hayrüddin, but the urbanism and feeling for geometrical order and architectural outline reveal the highest degree of scientific artistry. This monument on its hill glitters night and day like a diadem over the city of Istanbul.

61. Süleymaniye Mosque, side view. In this façade the space and constructional elements required by the plan have been reduced to order and harmony within the framework of a single surface. That is architecture. In this monument the dimensions and the effect created are no less magnificent than the Sultan Süleyman who caused it to be built.

The façade is 110·58 m. long; the dome is 27·44 m. wide and 47·42 m. above the ground, its peak is 5·30 m. wide; the minaret with three balconies is 68·30 m. high, or 76 m. inclusive of the pointed roof; its diameter at the base is 4 m. In the writer's opinion, the effect would have been better if the two other smaller minarets had been omitted. In installing four minarets Sinan's model was the Üç Şerefeli Mosque at Edirne.

62. Süleymaniye Mosque, interior. The architectural effect reflected in the outer façades is a product of this interior. The interior inscriptions are the work of Hasan Çelebi, the stained glass of İbrahim the Drunkard, and the tiles of the craftsmen of İznik. The area of the mosque is 3358·40 square metres. The internal acoustics are exceptionally good. This mosque is the work of a genius architect, 67 years of age.

63. Selimiye Mosque at Edirne. Sinan was 85 years old when he built this mosque. The proportions of the façade are of the modular order; in this way a mature beauty and rhythm have been produced. The lightening of the buttresses with niches and window-panels, the openwork lattices in the tympana of the arches over the windows, the deep shadows of the ground-floor arcades and the light shadows of the projecting gargoyles, the arrangement of numerous windows inside a large arch, the coloured stones, all contribute to a rich and attractive architecture, balanced and restful.

64. Selimiye Mosque, section. Externally, the mosque with its four minarets lifts towards the sky the hill on which it is set like a crown. These minarets, 70·89 m. high, or 82·90 m. with the conical roof, and 3.80 m. in diameter, are the tallest and slenderest in the Moslem world. The interior is spanned by a single dome 42·28 m. high and 31·27 m. in diameter; this dome is a marvel of statical technique. Here we see magnitude, height, space, colour and light combining, in perfect clarity, in an effect of superhuman beauty.

65. Selimiye Mosque, faiences. The base of the interior walls is veneered with faiences that rank among the finest works of Ottoman art in point of colour, design and workmanship.

66. Mihrimah Mosque at Istanbul, near the Adrianople Gate. Built by Rüstem Pasha, son-in-law and Grand Vizier of Süleyman the Magnificent, in memory of his wife, Mihrimah Sultan. For lack of a dating inscription the exact year of its construction is not known, but is generally placed between 1562 and 1565. This is one of the buildings that have been submitted to scrutiny in connection with Sinan's single-dome plan and building technique. Its single dome is supported on four arches and pillars. The spaces within these arches might well have been left empty; the walls, with many windows, that in fact fill them serve merely for enclosing the building. This building style is really a 'skeleton' system, and recalls the Gothic principle. To this extent only was the traditional massive form modernized and monumentalized. From work of this kind

the Selimiye Mosque was developed.

67. Sultan Ahmet Mosque at Istanbul. This mosque repeats the general plan of the Şehzade Mosque, but with certain innovations, as for example the interior and exterior galleries, the small half-domes supporting the four main half-domes, the round pillars and the brighter interior. No other mosque in the Turkish or Islamic world possesses six minarets. The dimensions are 64 by 72 m.

68. Interior view of the same mosque. The central dome measures 23·60 m., but gives the impression of more monumental proportions. The pillars are 5 m. in diameter, but appear slenderer by reason of their fluting and decoration; the round shape has the effect of gathering and unifying the interior space. The numerous windows not only provide a fine view, but also improve the visibility of the tiling that covers the walls.

69. Yeni Cami or Valide Mosque at Eminönü, Istanbul. The lighting shown in the photograph is modern. Traditionally, only the lamps on the balconies of the minarets are lit, and shine like a belt of light in the darkness. The Mahya, or texts formed by lamps suspended between the two minarets, are like a frame of stars in the sky. Similarly, in the interior the lamps hung from the domes form a low ceiling of lights, and reduce the majestic building to human proportions.

70. Same mosque, view from the courtyard. Here again the domes form a pyramidal outline, restful and harmonius. This mosque is the work not of one architect but of three,

and took 63 years to build, as compared with the normal five to seven years. It stood originally on a terrace by the shore; but the sea has now withdrawn and nothing remains of the original terrace.

71. Nuru Osmaniye Mosque at Istanbul. In Turkish Baroque style, whose weakness is that it applies to stone and marble curved forms which are more appropriate to plaster-work. It is to be noted, however, that it remains true to the classical Turkish plan-technique, architectural elements and general form. In particular, its monumental outline, reminiscent of the plastic form of the Mihrimah Mosque by the Adrianople Gate, is highly impressive.

72. Ortaköy Mosque at Istanbul. Built by Nikogos Balyan, one of Sultan Abdülmecit's architects, this mosque is a veritable gem and an ornament to the Bosporus. As in Europe, architecture is here treated more as a decorative than as a structural art.

73. Bostancı Mosque at Istanbul. Built by the architect Kemaleddin. The mosques at Bebek and Bakırköy, though externally different, are built on the same plan. The architecture of this mosque, which recalls the İznik and Bursa periods, may claim to represent the renaissance of classical Turkish art. Mosques of this kind, built of concrete, are pleasing, though not of monumental proportions; the dimensions here are 10·80 by 12·10 m., the dome is 5·40 m. high and 9·50 m. in diameter, the mosque is 10·99 m. high at the base of the dome, and the height of the minaret is 21 m.

74. Sırçalı Medrese at Konya. The

photograph shows the eyvan; though ruined, this gives a good idea of Seljuk tile-work. Of the students' rooms in the courtyard only two remain today.

75. Gateway of the same medrese. Among the decorative motifs may be noticed the rosettes, which afford opportunity for blank spaces in the ornamentation of the façade. This 'full-and-empty' technique is a peculiarity not found in other gateways.

76. Karatay Medrese at Konya. Built by an unknown architect to the orders of Emîr Celalüddin Karatay. Only the domed portion and the gateway survive. Its dimensions are approximately 24 m. by 32 m.; those of the gateway are 7·50 m. by 8·25 m. The multicoloured tile decoration of dome and walls, with its original designs, is of interest, as also is the form of the building.

77. Ince Minare at Konya. So called as being the tallest and slenderest minaret in Seljuk architecture. The shaft, composed of fascicles, is of coloured brick arranged in patterns. The distance between the two balconies was disproportionate; the upper part was unfortunately destroyed by lightning in 1899, and the effect is spoiled. The stone base has very handsome sculptured decoration. A noticeable feature is the colonnettes let into either side of the gateway; these are narrower at the bottom than at the top, and are decorated with fishes' scales. The gateway measures six by nine metres, and the whole building covers an area of 32·50 m. by 26·50 m.

78. Central dome of the same. This gives an excellent idea of the Seljuk building style. The brick material is so worked as to produce a handsome decoration with geometric designs.

79. Hatuniye Medrese at Erzurum, also called Çifte Minareli. The pillars of the courtyard, in Western Asiatic Seljuk style, show at the same time a remarkable resemblance to European Romanesque.

80. Yıldız Hatun Medrese at Amasya. The plan and structure of this building are adapted to its function as a mental disease clinic. The façade is considered plain by comparison with other Seljuk medreses. In Seljuk architecture mihrab, fountain and windows are each treated as a small portal; the same characteristic is observable in this façade.

81. Gök Medrese at Sivas. The fountains, built as works of charity, which are to be seen in the façade of some of the medreses at Kayseri and Konya, are found here also. The medrese itself is ruined and no longer dispenses learning; but the fountain in the front wall still distributes water to the populace. The sculptured decoration over the gateway, comprising various birds and animals' heads, is a noteworthy survival in Anatolia of the tradition of the Uygur animal calendar. The twin minarets are, in the writer's opinion, excessive; nor indeed is their relation to the gateway architecturally satisfying.

82. Câcâ Bey Medrese at Kırşehir. Built by Nuruddin Cibril bin Câcâ Bey, governor of Kırşehir, under Sultan Giyasüddin. Formerly a

medrese for meteorological observation, it is now used as a mosque. Its plan shows the transition from Seljuk to early Ottoman work. With its Seljuk gateway, minaret, türbe, brick and stone technique, architectural elements and decoration, this comparatively well-preserved building affords a unique opportunity for the simultaneous study of all the various features.

83. Ak Medrese at Niğde. This is a Karamanlı monument, as is shown by the form of the gateway, the ornamentation, the profile of the arches and mouldings, and the building material. The transitional cable motifs on the piers and arches that surround the courtyards show Central Asiatic influence—an influence largely promoted by the Ilhanlı artists who dominated Anatolia after the Seljuks. The building is important as affording a link between the Seljuk, Karamanlı and Ottoman Turkish traditions.

84. Muradiye Medrese at Bursa, beside the mosque and türbes of Sultan Murad II. Its courtyard plan and domed structure anticipate the classical Ottoman medrese, while the general layout, and the brick decoration, show little departure from the Seljuk type. For these reasons it is regarded as a transitional work. The recent restoration in 1952 has been successful in preserving its atmosphere and character as an ancient monument.

85. Mental Hospital and Mosque of Beyazıt II at Edirne. The geometric formation of this social welfare group of buildings, the monumental architecture in squared stone, and above all the cubic plastic effect of the mosque, distinguish it from the Bursa school. We have now reached the threshold of the classical Ottoman period.

86. Particulars of the Mental Hospital, now in ruins. As may be seen, the architecture, the technique, and the acoustic arrangements are a veritable marvel. The dome of the auditorium measures externally not more than 14·93 m. The modest dimensions and proportions are intended to enhance the structural dominance of the mosque. The architect, in the plan as in the elevation, has observed a sense of proportion and the basic principles of town-planning.

87. Medrese of Beyazıt II at Istanbul. The façades, of squared stone, are quiet and plain; the only variety is afforded by the stone-and-brick walls of the covered classroom block. Thus, the Bursa tradition lives on, and is accentuated here by the resemblance to the Green Medrese. The interior courtyard, with its green trees and şadırvan, has the calm and restful atmosphere of the city-landscapes of Turkistan.

88. Selimiye Boys' School at Edirne. Primary schools are no less important architecturally than medreses. They have a single-doomed classrom on the upper floor; in the present case there is an open-air terrace in front of the classroom, a noteworthy feature, to which importance is attached in modern school architecture in Switzerland and England. The forms and material are characteristic of the period.

89. Döner Kümbet at Kayseri. In form this building recalls the old Turkish

tent; it has also something in common with Kurgan, Tope and Tomba. Its dimensions, however, are more modest; it rises 14·20 m. on a base of 7·50 m. Its conical stone roof rests on a cylindrical cornice, from which the transition to the dodecagonal main body is effected by means of blind arcades. Several steps lead to the entrance; the cylindrical interior is roofed with a dome adorned with a cornice.

90. Mausoleum of Melik Gazi at Kırşehir. The adaptation to stone of the tent form is here more evident. The conical stone roof is reminiscent of the pointed felt caps worn by the peasants.

91. Hudabend Kümbet at Niğde. The majestic doorway is notable for its decorative sculpture. This building, like the Döner Kümbet, is adorned with a series of figures.

92. Mausolea at Erzurum and Ahlat. One of these is the türbe added to the Çifte Minareli Medrese at Erzurum; the other is the türbe of Emîr Bayındır at Ahlat. The blind arcades which are found above the cylindrical body in the türbes of Erzurum and Kayseri are here left open. Apart from the details of the architectural forms, these two buildings may be said to exhibit the same conception and spirit.

93. Türbe of Çelebi Mehmet at Bursa. A transitional work. The character of the Ottoman türbe has taken definite shape, and decoration and colour have been extended to the interior. Yet the Seljuk tradition is also evident; the dome is parabolic in form, and the external façades contain tiled surfaces. From the colour of the tiles this building is called the Green Türbe. It is one of the monuments that give Bursa its character.

94. Türbe of Murad II at Bursa. This building has certain characteristics of the Bursa School, notably the alternate stone and brick courses of the façades, the marble gateway, and the prominence given to the eaves. The eaves of the gateway, with their star patterns and geometric motifs, are a marvel of wood-carving. The plain yet significant form of the building is inspired by the türbes of Orhan and Murad I. The four columns taken from ancient ruins, and the capitals turned upside down to serve as bases, have a symbolic meaning.

95. Muradiye Türbes at Bursa. These türbes are set in the peaceful, other-world atmosphere of a cemetery shaded by cypress and plane-trees. The türbe of Gülşah Hatun in the foreground of the photograph is architecturally more archaic than the others. The picture shows the türbe of Karaca Bey at Ankara, included here for comparison to illustrate the relation between the Ottoman türbes of the mid-fifteenth century and the sepulchral architecture associated with Bursa.

96. Şehzade Türbe at Istanbul. The old Turkish building tradition still survives in this work of the mid-sixteenth century, but at the same time we see that the Ottoman türbe has attained its classical architectural form. Prince Mehmet, in the türbe where he was buried after his tragic death, strives as it were, amid the colourful arrangement of

106

the tiled panels, to prolong the springtime of his life.

97. Türbe of Barbarossa at Istanbul (1541). An example of the pure Ottoman türbe type. This building of squared stone, with its simple monumental effect, is a fitting memorial to the Turkish admiral who was the terror of the Mediterranean. It is situated at Beşiktaş, on the shore of the sea that he knew so well in life.

98. Nakşidil Sultan's Türbe at Istanbul. The softness of the marble-veneered exterior, together with the rich and colourful interior decoration, make this monument of Turkish Baroque highly appropriate to a woman Sultan; it is indeed a model of grace and beauty. Its sebil is visible beside it.

99. Türbe of Fuad Pasha at Istanbul. Here Turkish architecture is seen to have entered a purely decorative stage; in Ottoman, as in all other architecture, the zenith was followed by a decline. By a later reaction the Ottoman renaissance was to bring back the beauty of the classical türbe.

100. Ağzıkara Han, on the Kayseri–Aksaray road. Begun by Alâüddin Keykûbâd and finished in 1231 by his son, Keyhüsrev II. In plan it is of the Sultan Khan (or Caravanserai) type, with mescit in the courtyard; it is in a good stage of preservation. In particular, the contrast between the decorative sculptured gateway and the solid walls of squared stone in which it is set is well brought out in the photograph. This contrast is considered the essential characteristic of Seljuk architecture.

101. Sultan Khan, on the Aksaray–Konya road. This interior view shows the covered hall, or winter quarters; the dimensions and the architectural effect are equally impressive. The approximate measurements are: exterior length 119 m., front 53 m.; total area 4,350 sq. m. The covered portion, about 1,500 sq. m., is narrower than the courtyard portion. Some architects regard this as a masterpiece of Seljuk art.

102. Bey Khan at Bursa. This is the earliest work exhibiting the type of the Ottoman commercial khan. The restoration attempted here gives a good idea of the building. The asymmetrical façade is very simple and attractive; its Bursa School features and medieval character are evident.

103. Khan of Rüstem Pasha at Edirne, a work of Sinan. In the sixteenth-century khans the Bursa tradition continues, as appears from the shape of the arches and piers in the galleries, the alternate use of stone and brick in the wall surface, and the general planning technique. The abstract design in brickwork over the window will give pleasure to non-figurative artists.

104. Simkeşhane (Silver Thread factory) at Istanbul. The plan and the façades were characteristic specimens of Turkish civil architecture. The photograph gives an idea of the structure of the khans at Istanbul.

105. Vakıf Khan IV, at Istanbul. Early in the present century, architects were in the habit of applying to European building-plans the façades of the Ottoman architecture. This

H*

was a step towards a renaissance; but this style, being unsuited to reinforced concrete technique and other new inventions, had a short life.

106. Bedesten of Mahmut Pasha at Ankara. In the photograph the low-roofed portion in the block seen in the foreground indicates the market. The domed portion rising in the middle indicates the covered hall of the bedesten, measuring 18 m. by 49 m.; this is lit from above by windows let into the walls of the bedesten behind the roof of the market. It was restored in 1935. It is interesting to observe the manner in which the Kurşunlu Han in the upper part is set into the ground.

107. 'Egyptian' Market at Istanbul. Now used as a covered market-hall. Its architecture is rational: the windows in the sides of the high, sloping-roofed central portion give light to the central passage inside. This passage, on a lower level, forms a right-angle on either side of which are set the rows of shops, 88 in all, each covered by a dome. The building is of a single storey, except over the entrance arcades, where an upper floor contains the managerial offices.

108. 'Egyptian' Market, interior. The effect is as impressive as that of a cathedral; but the dimensions are more modest. The pointed tunnel-vault in the middle, 10 m. high, rests on stone arches 0·90 m. wide, set 3·80 m. apart. In front of the shops the pointed-arched eyvans, 6·30 m. high and 1·75 m. deep, were used for buying and selling; the covered part behind served as a depôt. The building was restored in 1944.

109. Palace of Kılıçarslan II at Konya, no longer in existence. The photograph, taken some 50 years ago, illustrates the various elements of Seljuk architecture, e.g. form of arch, consoles, tiled window-frames, etc. Many fragments of glazed tiles found during excavations on the site give some idea of the size and ornamentation of the palace.

110. Çinili Köşk at Istanbul. This is the oldest and most important monument of the Ottoman capital. It is a transitional work illustrating, in respect of form, decoration and technique, the Turkish architectural tradition which began with the Seljuks of Horasan and Anatolia, developed at Bursa, and finally passed to Istanbul.

111. Gateway of the Topkapı Palace at Istanbul. The Middle Gate, giving access to the second court of the palace, is in the same spirit as the gate of Horsâbâd Palace, and resembles a castle gate. The simple and solid architecture, and the towers with their pointed roofs, are a symbol of the power securing the defence and safety of the palace; they are at the same time highly attractive.

112. Baghdad Pavilion at Istanbul. This gem of Ottoman architecture was built to the order of Sultan Murad IV to immortalize the victory of Baghdad. To protect the graceful and delicate building the arcades have been filled in, on the side exposed to the wind, with a modern iron window-grating; this spoils the architectural harmony and effect.

113. Baghdad Pavilion, interior. The effect is even richer and more

impressive than the exterior. In this one interior we find all the colour and ornamentation of Ottoman architecture. The stained-glass panels, the woodwork of windows and door inlaid with mother-of-pearl, the polychrome designs that adorn the dome, the artistic script along the freize, and the metalwork of the bronze hearth, together form a veritable exhibition of Turkish decorative art.

114. Pavilion of Mustafa Pasha at Istanbul, close to the Baghdad Pavilion. A cool and airy summer-house, built of wood. The furniture and windows conform to Turkish traditions; only the style of decoration is different and exhibits innovations.

115. Bedroom of Murad III (1574–1595), in the Topkapı Palace at Istanbul. This room gives an impression of the harem of an Ottoman palace. All the branches of Turkish art, faience, decorative script, marble, woodwork, bronze and stained glass, are here assembled as if in a museum. These adornments relieve the heavy and shut-in atmosphere of this interior, which however was essential to the intimate life of the harem. This is the most handsome tiled room of the harem.

116. Palace of Ahmet I at Istanbul, outside the city, in front of the Davut Pasha barracks. It is a plain building of squared stone, in two storeys with vaults and domes. The plan recalls the T-shape of the İznik and Bursa tradition. It was badly ruined, but was saved by restoration in 1946.

117. Aynalı Kavak Pavilion at Istanbul. Of the old Dockyard Palace and gardens on the Golden Horn nothing

remains today. The pavilion got its name from the large mirrors, tall as poplar trees, presented by the Venetians after 1715 and placed in it by the Sultan. The present pavilion was built later by Selim III. The plan and façades are true to tradition, yet display a new architectural conception.

118. Dolmabahçe Palace at Istanbul. Built by Sultan Mecid in place of the old Beşiktaş Palace which he knocked down. The architectural style, heavy and highly ornamental, is in accordance with nineteenth-century taste. The higher central portion is the hall of ceremonies; the harem extends to the right of this, the Sultan's quarters to the left. Altogether there are 200 rooms. The building material is costly and the workmanship highly artistic. The total cost was 5,000,000 gold pounds. Of the historical events that have taken place within it the most melancholy was the funeral of Atatürk.

119. House of Murad II at Bursa. So called, though it cannot be more than 300 years old. The building is in two storeys, open towards the garden but not towards the street. the living-rooms are on the upper floor; downstairs are the servants' quarters. Special features are the veranda, the outside staircase and the richness of the interior. The restoration is not, in the writer's opinion, successful, giving the impression of a new building rather than an ancient monument.

120. Red Yalı at Istanbul. A survival of seventeenth‑century architecture on the shores of the Bosporus. The

window strips, embracing a view of the sea on all sides, are paralleled only in European works of the present century. The building is not of stone, it is not monumental, and its character is quite different from that of religious architecture; but this makes it all the more successful. To suit the material and form to the purpose of the building is the true function of architecture.

121. Yalı at Emirgân, Istanbul. Here again we find traditional Bosporus architecture, except that the style shows a certain Baroque tendency.

122. Yalı of Köçeoğlu at Istanbul. These pictures show that in the domestic architecture of the nineteenth century the principle of conformity to the landscape and style of construction is still observed. This building, like many others, has unfortunately been pulled down in the course of widening the road. In its place modern concrete apartments are being built, but these are lacking in character. The poetry of the old Bosporus architecture is now a historical memory.

123. Eski Kaplıca at Bursa. That this is a genuine work of Ottoman architecture was sufficiently demonstrated above. It is a mistake to regard it as Byzantine. True, Byzantine column capitals have been used in it; but this is due to economical reasons and the desire of a conquering nation to use the spoils it has taken from the conquered as a souvenir. The Turkish builders, for this reason, like those of the Middle Ages, were tempted to use in almost all their buildings the ancient architectural elements that they found to hand.

124. Haseki Baths at Istanbul, between St. Sophia and the Sultan Ahmet Mosque. Built by Sinan to the orders of Hurrem Sultan. Of all the baths in Istanbul this is the largest and most impressive work of urban architecture. To solve the problems of height and space which are set by the differing requirements of the various rooms, and to produce from these an effective exterior, calls for the highest architectural skill.

125. Fountain of Sahib Atâ at Konya, at the gate of the mosque. Just 700 years old, it gives an idea of the Seljuk fountain. The original idea of applying to fountains the form of door- or window-arches was bequeathed by the Seljuks to the Ottomans.

126. Fountain of Sultan Ahmet at Istanbul. Combined fountain-and-sebil type. The effect is monumental, and marks the transition of Ottoman architecture to the Rococo period.

127. Üsküdar Fountain at Istanbul, in the square by the boat station. Built originally by Sultan Ahmet III in 1728, it has four façades and is veneered with marble on all sides. In consequence of later repairs, the decoration of the roof and eaves is not in harmony with that of the original classical Ottoman portion below. The photograph was taken while repairs were in progress, so that the building is partially obscured. Dimensions are 7·40 by 7·40 by 5·00 m.

128. Sebil at Lâleli, Istanbul. A round marble building erected by Sultan Mustafa III. The five openings between the six columns have wrought-iron railings, in the lower

110

part of which small arched openings are left for the issue of water to the populace. This is a handsome and graceful Ottoman work of the Rococo period.

129. Şadırvan of Beyazıt II at Istanbul, in the inner courtyard of the Beyazıt Medrese. The highly original form of this building culminates in a pointed roof; this latter feature is inherited from Anatolian Seljuk architecture. The surrounding trees combine with the cool water to give an air of peacefulness. The Turkish custom of adorning courtyards with trees and water derives from a very ancient tradition going back to the cities of Turkistan.

130. Rumeli Hisarı, Istanbul. This castle was built by Mehmet the Conqueror in 1452, one year before the capture of the city. Conforming to the nature of the ground and the strategic conditions, it covers an area 250 by 125 m., and forms a veritable hill city in miniature. The towers formerly had conical roofs. In form and construction it is reminiscent of western fortification works. The sketch is included to give an idea of Turkish military architecture, for which no space could be found in the severely restricted text of the present work.

INDEX

35. KONYA. Alâüddin Mosque

36. KONYA. Alâüddin Mosque,

a. interior,

b. mihrab and dome

37. DİVRİĞİ. Ulu Cami and Mental Hospital

38. DİVRİĞİ. Mental Hospital, interior

39. KASTAMONU. Mosque of Mahmut Bey, interior and detail of ceiling

40. Bursa. Ulu Cami, interior

41. BURSA. Ulu Cami, şadırvan

42. İZNİK. Green (yeşil) Mosque

43. Bursa. Murad Hüdavendigâr Mosque-Medrese, restored elevation

BURSA YILDIRIM CAMİİ CEPHESİ

44. BURSA. Yıldırım Mosque, elevation

45. BURSA. Yıldırım Mosque,
side views

46. BURSA. Green (yeşil) Mosque, general view and detail of façade

47. Bursa. Green Mosque, rear view

48. Bursa. Green Mosque, mihrab

49. BURSA. Green Mosque, Sultan's balcony

50. EDİRNE. Old Mosque

51. EDİRNE. Üç Şerefeli Mosque: note flying buttresses

52. Edİrne. Üç Şerefeli Mosque, entrance and court

53. ISTANBUL. Fâtih (the Conqueror)
    Mosque

54. ISTANBUL. Fâtih Mosque, court and şadırvan

55. ISTANBUL. Beyazıt II Mosque, general view

56. ISTANBUL. Beyazıt II Mosque, gateway into court

57. ISTANBUL. Şehzade Mosque, side elevation

58. ISTANBUL. Şehzade Mosque

59. ELBİSTAN. Ulu Cami. Note: Earliest example of dome and half dome in conjunction
with diagonal buttresses

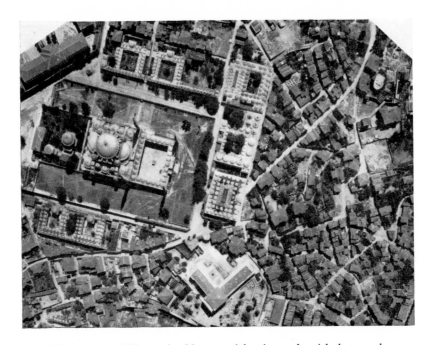

60. ISTANBUL. Süleymaniye Mosque, night view and aerial photograph

61. ISTANBUL. Süleymaniye Mosque, side elevation

62. ISTANBUL. Süleymaniye Mosque, interior

63. EDİRNE. Selimiye Mosque

64. EDİRNE. Selimiye Mosque, longitudinal section showing the great space spanned
with a single dome, unequalled for size

65. EDIRNE. Selimiye Mosque, wall faience

66. ISTANBUL. Mihrimah Mosque, example of masonry frame

67. ISTANBUL. Sultan Ahmet Mosque, aerial photograph, with St. Sophia in the background

68. Istanbul. Sultan Ahmet Mosque, interior

69. ISTANBUL. Yeni Cami, night view

70. Istanbul. Yeni Cami, court and şadırvan

71. ISTANBUL. Nuru Osmaniye Mosque,
gate and general view

72. ISTANBUL. Ortaköy Mosque

73. ISTANBUL. Bostancı Mosque, classic revival

74. KONYA. Sırçalı Medrese, courtyard and eyvan

75. KONYA. Sırçalı Medrese, gateway

76. KONYA. Ruins of Karatay Medrese. The lantern in the dome and the gateway roof are later additions

77. KONYA. Ince Minare, general view and details

78. KONYA. İnce Minare, dome and pendentives, a skilful use of bricks

79. ERZURUM. Hatuniye Medrese, court

80. AMASYA. Yıldız Hatun Medrese, or Mental Hospital

81. SİVAS. Gök Medrese, gateway

82. KIRSEHİR. Câcâ Bey Medrese

83. Niğde. Ak Medrese, court

84. Bursa. Muradiye Medrese, restored elevation and section

85. EDİRNE. Beyazıt II Mosque and Mental Hospital

86. EDİRNE. Beyazıt II Mental Hospital, reconstructed

87. ISTANBUL. Beyazıt II Medrese

88. EDİRNE. Selimiye Boys' School

89. KAYSERİ. Döner Kümbet (Mausoleum).
Note the harmony with the landscape

90. KIRSEHİR. Mausoleum of Melik Gazi

91. NİĞDE. Hudabend Kümbet

92. AHLAT, ERZURUM. Mausolea

93. BURSA. Green Mausoleum,
general view and tiled niche

94. BURSA. Türbe of Murad II, eaves and entrance

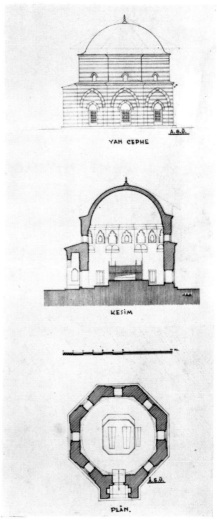

YAN CEPHE

KESİM

PLÂN.

95. *a*. BURSA. Muradiye Mausolea
b. ANKARA. Karaca Bey Türbe,
plan, section and elevation

96. ISTANBUL. Türbe of Şehzade Mehmet

97. ISTANBUL. Türbe of Barbarossa Hayreddin Pasha

98. ISTANBUL. Türbe of Nakşidil Sultan

99. ISTANBUL. Türbe of Fuad Pasha, example of eclectic style

100. KAYSERİ. Agzıkara Inn

101. KONYA-AKSARAY, Sultan Khan. interior view

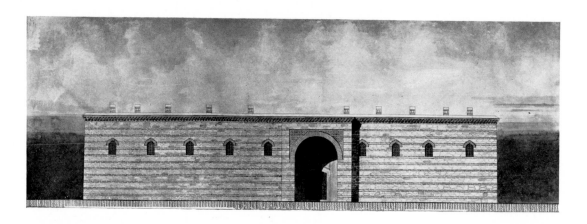

102. BURSA. Bey Khan, restored elevation and section

103. EDİRNE. Rüstem Pasha Khan, gallery of courtyard and detail of masonry

104. ISTANBUL. Simkeşhane

105. ISTANBUL. Vakıf Khan

106. ANKARA. Sketch of Mahmut Pasha Bedesten

107. ISTANBUL. Mısır Çarşısı, after restoration

108. ISTANBUL. Mısır Çarsısı, interior

109. KONYA. Ruins of Palace of Kılıçarslan II

110. ISTANBUL. Çinili Köşk, after restoration

111. ISTANBUL. Topkapı Palace, First and
Middle gateways

112. ISTANBUL. Baghdad Pavilion, in the Topkapı Palace

113. Istanbul. Baghdad Pavilion, interior

114. ISTANBUL. Mustafa Pasha Pavilion in Topkapı Palace

115. ISTANBUL. Bedroom of Murad III, in Topkapı Palace

116. ISTANBUL. Davut Pasha Palace

117. ISTANBUL. Aynalı Kavak Pavilion, exterior and interior

118. ISTANBUL. Dolmabahçe Palace, general view

119. BURSA. House of Murad II, from the courtyard after restoration

120. ISTANBUL. Red yalı (Hüseyin Pasha yalısı)

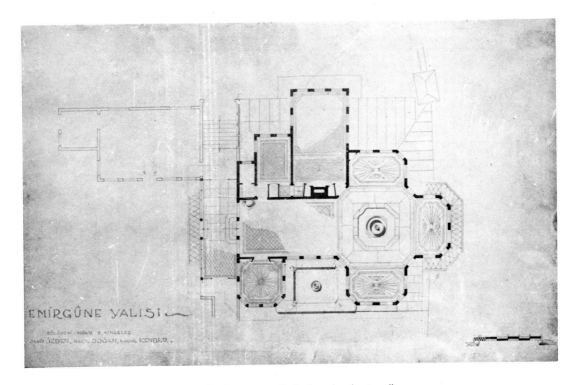

121. ISTANBUL. Emirgân yalısı (restored)

122. ISTANBUL. Köçeoğlu yalısı

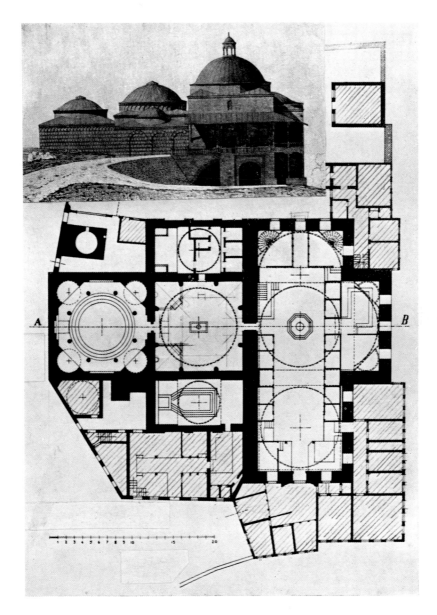

123. BURSA. Eski Kaplıca (hot springs), restored plan and elevation

124. ISTANBUL. Haseki Baths, for men and women

125. KONYA. One of the two Sahib Atâ fountains, side flanking Mosque gateway

126. ISTANBUL. Sultan Ahmet public fountain

127. ISTANBUL. Public fountain at Üsküdar

128. ISTANBUL. Lâleli Sebili

129. ISTANBUL. Şadırvan of Beyazıt II Medrese

130. ISTANBUL. Rumeli Hisarı (castle)